NICK

Happy Christmas

taken relaxa

Love Annie X

G000071328

A Fly-Fishing Life

Books by William G. Tapply

A Fly-Fishing Life

William G. Tapply

Distributed by:
Airlife Publishing Ltd
101 Longden Road, Shrewsbury SY3 9EB, England

Printed in the United States of America

10   9   8   7   6   5   4   3   2   1

Design by Jennifer Corsano

Library of Congress Cataloging-in-Publication Data
Tapply, William G.
A fly-fishing life / William G. Tapply.
p.   cm.
ISBN 1-55821-544-1
1. Fly fishing—Anecdotes. 2. Tapply, William G. I. Title.
SH456.T355   1997
799.1′24′092—dc21   97-23809   CIP

Some of these stories have appeared in the following publications:
*Field & Stream, American Angler, Yankee, The Boston Globe Magazine,
Gray's Sporting Journal, Saltwater Fly Fishing, Fly Fisherman,
Saltwater Sportsman, Worcester Magazine,* and *Angler's Journal*

Dedication

I've had the good fortune to share this fly-fishing life with more like-minded companions than any man has a right to expect. Dad took me with him as soon as I proved I could be "seen and not heard," and his friends tolerated—and sometimes seemed actually to welcome—my presence. So I got to fish with such deservedly famous experts as Lee Wulff and Harold Blaisdell, as well as Dad's anonymous friends, many of whom were also experts.

Fly-fishing guides have given me more than the locations of worthy fish and the strategies for catching them. Several of them—Bill Rohrbacher in particular—appear as important characters in these pages because my times with them have been memorable, regardless of the fish we've caught.

For the past decade or so, I've shared rental cars and float planes and driftboats and poker tables with a group of men who have enriched my time on—and off—the water beyond measure. They've inspired me to write about it, and they've tried to hold me to the truth of it. This book is dedicated to these treasured friends—Steve Cooper, Jon Kolb, Andy Gill, Randy Paulsen, and Elliot Schildkrout—with the prayer that they will continue to share this fly-fishing life with me as long as we all can wade and cast and pour bourbon into a glass and toss chips onto a felt-topped table.

Out Fishin'

by Edgar A. Guest

A feller isn't thinkin' mean,
　　Out fishin';
His thoughts are mostly good an' clean,
　　Out fishin';
He doesn't knock his fellow men
　　Or harbor any grudges then;
A feller's at his finest, when
　　Out fishin'.

The rich are comrades to the poor,
　　Out fishin';
All brothers of a common lure
　　Out fishin';
The urchin with the pin an' string
　　Can chum with millionaire an' king;
Vain pride is a forgotten thing,
　　Out fishin'.

A feller's glad to be a friend,
　　Out fishin';
A helping hand he'll always lend,
　　Out fishin';
The brotherhood of rod and line
　　An' sky an' stream is always fine;
Men come real close to God's design
　　Out fishin'.

CONTENTS

Introduction

Time on the Water

Of the fishermen he observed on the banks of Walden Pond, Thoreau said: "Commonly [they] did not think that they were lucky, or well paid for their time, unless they got a long string of fish, though they had the opportunity of seeing the pond all the while. They might go there a thousand times before the sediment of fishing would sink to the bottom and leave their purpose pure; but no doubt such a clarifying process would be going on all the while."

I haunted Walden when I was a kid. I fished for trout with worms, which I lobbed into the water with an old hand-me-down fly rod. Stillfishing this way required a high tolerance for waiting, and I discovered that I had a certain gift for it. I was never bored, never felt that I was wasting time, and while I was always hopeful that a fish would come along and pick up my bait, I found plenty to do while I squatted on Walden's rock-cobbled shores. Long before I began to read Thoreau, I learned, although I could not have begun to articulate it back then, that fishing is a "clarifying process." This process continues still, although even now, forty-odd years later, my purpose is still not entirely pure.

I've gone fishing thousands of times in my life, and I have never once felt unlucky or poorly paid for all those hours on the water. I've willingly confronted what, to others, might seem like intolerable discomfort and even danger for the chance to catch a fish, and I've been skunked more than my share of times. But my time on the water has never been wasted. I've had ponds and rivers and saltwater flats to entertain and teach me every time.

I fish hard and often—primarily, though not exclusively, with the fly rod. Although my homely local places continue to fascinate me, I also travel great distances to fish, and I have little desire to travel anywhere that I cannot fish. I arise before the sun to be on the water, and sometimes I linger there long after night falls. I endure mosquitoes and blackflies, rain and snow, blasting Montana heat and frigid New England winters, with no thought of complaint.

I love to fish. When I cannot fish, I think about fishing. I tie flies and read books about fishing. I correspond with fishermen all over the country. Most of my close friends are fishing partners. I cannot imagine not fishing. I would not be me if I did not fish.

Even as the sediment of fishing has begun to clear and catching fish has become less important to me, I find that I have gotten better at it. I have learned to slow down and pay attention to the way water moves and insects reproduce and fish behave. I have watched and listened to other fishermen. I have tried to learn the hard lessons that fish teach.

Luckily, there's still a lot I don't know. Every day on the water teaches me something. If that should ever change, I suspect my passion for fishing would diminish disturbingly.

I still live close to Walden, and I still go there in April with a fly rod and a can of worms, and while I sometimes think Transcendental Thoughts while hunkering on the bank waiting for a trout to come along, mostly I just wait for my line to twitch and begin slithering out through the guides. I still hunt down hidden brooks where the trout are small and wild and the best way to catch them is on a worm. I have traveled far to cast for tarpon and permit and chinook salmon and Atlantic salmon, but I still like to roll up my pant legs and wade the weedy shorelines of my local ponds, casting little foam poppers against the lily pads for bluegills.

I began as a toddler, hanging a worm under a bobber and catching panfish from the Charles River. I passed through what I'm told are the classic stages: First I wanted to catch a fish, and then many fish, and then large fish, and then fish of certain desirable species, and then difficult fish. Along the way, I learned that the way I liked best to do those things was with a fly rod, and I learned to treasure every minute I spent on the water regardless of how many fish I caught. But I never stopped wanting to catch fish, nor did I stop fishing with worms or loving panfish.

For me, becoming a fly fisherman has been a matter of adding layers, not passing through stages. I began with bluegills and largemouth bass, and I pursue them still. Then I got hooked on the mysteries of trout, and my passion for them continues to grow. Lately, great schools of striped bass have returned to our New England creeks and estuaries. They have given me new and delicious mysteries to investigate, complex equations of tide and moon and sun and season to puzzle over, and they drag me from my bed at strange hours without a whimper.

But if there are eels or suckers to be caught, I will fish for them, and if a fly rod won't do the job, I'll try a handline. I am still all the other fishermen I have ever been.

These stories are my way of exploring what all those hours on the water—particularly, but not exclusively, those I've spent fly fishing—have meant to me throughout my life, and how my fishing continues to shape and define me. This is not a technical how-to book, although some of the lessons the fish have taught me are contained in it. Nor is it abstract or esoteric. It's mostly autobiographical and anecdotal. It's about people and places, fish and insects, success and failure, growing up and growing old. It's a book about love and passion and a life's journey in search of meaning. It's a book about the sediment—what settles to the bottom, the weighty, important stuff that's left when you take away the fishing.

All of these stories have, in some form, been published before, and the editors who printed them always insisted that I get them right. In the process, these editors have taught me a lot about writing—which, like fly fishing, is an occupation that repeatedly refutes the theory of the perfectibility of man.

I have tweaked these stories a few more times, as I cannot seem to resist doing. I know I'll never write the perfect story, any more than I'll master fly fishing. But I will keep trying to do both.

Good editors are, by definition, good writers and good teachers. My dad, H. G. "Tap" Tapply, was an editor, and I've been learning about writing—as well as fishing—from him for half a century. I've been lucky to work with good and demanding editors throughout my career, especially Duncan Barnes and Slaton White at *Field & Stream* and Art Scheck at *American Angler*. And every fishing writer who's ever had the good fortune to know Nick Lyons will tell you that he is, simply, the best.

I

Stillfishing, After All These Years

We may say of angling as Dr. Boteler said of strawberries: "Doubtless God could have made a better berry, but doubtless God never did"; and so, if I might be judge, God never did make a more calm, quiet, innocent recreation than angling.

—Izaak Walton, *The Compleat Angler*

1

Wasting Time at the Old Res

The Old Res was an abandoned reserve water reservoir for the eastern Massachusetts suburb where I grew up. It covered only a few surface acres. It was shallow and weedy, and it smelled of wet mud and decaying vegetation and dead fish.

No one fished at the Old Res except me.

The little pond nestled in a tree-lined bowl a three-minute walk over the hill behind my house, and it held many fascinations for a boy. It was a complex stew of unglamorous fish: pumpkinseeds, bluegills, crappies, yellow perch, horned pout, shiners. There were some small pickerel and an occasional eel, and rumors—never confirmed—of more exotic species. Bullfrogs and crawfish lived there, too, and snapping turtles the size of washtubs. Neon dragonflies and damselflies liked to perch on a rod tip. Herons sometimes high-stepped among the cattails, and most years a pair of mallards raised a family at the Old Res. On a summer evening swallows dipped and darted over the water, and when there were bugs on the surface fish swirled at them, leaving rings that, to my imagination, looked more substantial than any ever made by a stunted bluegill. I had no trouble convincing myself that a four-pound largemouth or two lived there, or maybe a lunker brown trout.

I read the outdoor magazines. I knew that great fish came from unlikely places. I knew that a fisherman's grandest accomplishment was to catch a trophy from a place where no one believed any trophy lived.

Naturally, I haunted the Old Res.

I threaded a gob of worms onto a hook and lobbed it into the murky waters of the Old Res. Then I propped my rod—it was one of my father's old bamboo fly rods with a repaired tip section—in a forked stick. I scooched on the bank and waited for the inevitable twitch and jerk out there at the end of my line. I believed that next twitch and jerk could be caused by a four-pound largemouth, and the fact that it never happened didn't shake my faith.

I always carried a box of Dad's hand-me-down trout flies with me, and whenever I ran out of worms, or just wanted to do something different, I practiced fly casting. Those little sunfish and crappies splashed at my bushy bivisibles and Wulffs no matter how sloppily I heaved them out there, and so, in the most natural possible way, I became a fly fisherman.

When I got tired of fishing, I waded in the shallows and tried to catch crawfish and painted turtles and frogs with my hands. I watched swallows snag mosquitoes and herons spear sunfish. I identified the muskrat and coon tracks on the mud banks. On hot afternoons I shucked off my clothes and skinny-dipped in the Old Res, then sprawled on the grass and napped naked under the sun.

So I spent the endless days of a boy's summer wandering and exploring and lazing around on the muddy banks of the Old Res. I learned how to enjoy my own company while staring at the place where my line dipped into the water, and although I couldn't have explained it, I learned about freedom.

Then came the year when my parents decided I was old enough to go off to summer camp, and for a month I lived by a rigid schedule of organized "group activities": sports and games, arts and crafts, swimming and archery lessons. Wandering and exploring and lazing around were not included in the camp curriculum. Neither was fishing. I couldn't wait to get back to the Old Res.

The same afternoon that I returned home from camp I dug some worms, grabbed my rod and a box of flies, and hurried over the hill to my pond.

When I pushed through the bushes that bordered its banks, I found an adult fisherman standing there cranking a spinning reel. He had an old-fashioned wicker creel slung over his shoulder. And then I saw other grown-up fishermen, dozens of them, spaced out around the entire circumference of the Old Res.

I felt a surge of panic. Something was terribly wrong. Why would a bunch of adults want to catch perch and sunfish out of my muddy little pond?

"How're they biting?" I asked the guy with the spinning outfit, trying to sound casual.

He turned and smiled at me. "Pretty good. This is a good spot." He tapped his creel. "I got three nice ones so far."

I didn't want to know, but I had to ask. "What kind of nice ones?"

"Well, trout, of course."

The man must have read my expression, because he explained that a couple of weeks earlier the state had added the

Old Res to its list of stocked waters and had dumped in a truck-load of hatchery brook trout.

So I lost my private place. The state continued to stock it regularly, and the Old Res became known and popular. Fly fishermen in chest waders cast graceful loops over the water, and spin fishermen heaved shiny lures far beyond the places where I'd lobbed gobs of worms. Families ate picnics and listened to portable radios on its grassy banks. Little kids splashed in the shallows chasing crawfish, and I never again found solitude or freedom at the Old Res.

I went there a few more times and caught some of those hatchery trout. Once I even caught one while casting a bivisible with my tip-shortened fly rod. But it was never the same, and after a while I stopped fishing at the Old Res altogether.

In my heart I absolutely believed that if I had stayed home instead of going to camp that summer, none of it would have happened.

I told myself that I didn't care, that the Old Res was too near-by and too lacking in mystery for me anyway, that I was too old to wander and explore and laze around at a shallow, weedy, smelly old backyard pond, that I had outgrown the thrill of catching a stunted horned pout on a gob of worms. I told myself that my time had become too valuable to waste doing those things.

I told myself that I wasn't a kid anymore.

And so, inevitably, I became an angler. I spurned shallow muddy ponds that harbored only small, unglamorous fish. I traveled long distances in quest of exotic species—trout, steelhead, bonefish, tarpon, permit, Pacific salmon—and it wasn't until it came time to introduce my son to fishing that I returned to a little neighborhood pond much like the Old Res.

I strung up one of my old fly rods, impaled a worm on a hook, showed him how to lob it out there, and my boy and I sat on the grassy bank waiting for the line to twitch and jerk. Dragonflies perched on the rod, and we spied on herons and ducks and kingfishers. When we got tired of fishing we shucked off our shoes, rolled up our pant legs, and waded the shallows, hunting crawfish and turtles and frogs. We looked for coon and muskrat tracks in the mud.

I gave my son his first fly-casting lesson at that little pond. Bluegills splashed at the bivisible he dumped out there, and he caught a few of them.

And gradually it occurred to me that the tepid water of the Old Res had been coursing through my veins all the time.

2

The Sediment of Fishing

I learned the contours of Walden's shoreline long before I studied Thoreau's map. I measured its depths not through a hole in the ice with a cod-line and stone, as he did, but from the shore with a fishing line and baited hook. I gradually learned the submerged points and bars and dropoffs where trout waited to gobble a worm, and I mapped them in my head, not on paper.

When I couldn't talk my mother into driving me there, I would spend an hour pedaling my bicycle to Walden. The Old Res, my weedy panfish pond, was just a short walk from my back door. Walden's distance made it alluring. Besides, it held only trout, and some of them grew big. When my line twitched from my rod tip at Walden, I knew it was caused by a magical fish.

And so I haunted Walden as a kid. Time seemed to be a limitless resource, and I spent it lavishly at Thoreau's pond. I brought one of my father's hand-me-down fly rods and a box of bait hooks and a Campbell's soup can of freshly dug earthworms. I cut a forked stick from an alder sapling and drove it into the gravel at the water's edge. I impaled a gob of worms onto my hook, lobbed it out as far as I could, let it sink to the bottom, and propped my rod in the forked stick.

Then I crouched there, staring intently at the tip of my rod, focusing the full power of my will on it to make it quiver and twitch and to start the line slithering out through the guides. When staring at the rod tip didn't work, I pretended to ignore it, on the theory that trout were most likely to bite when they thought you weren't paying attention. I whittled points onto the ends of sticks with my Boy Scout knife. On a chilly April morning I built a hand-warming fire from the shavings and pointed sticks, and if that didn't work, I stood up, stretched, and ostentatiously turned my back on my rod. I wandered along the shore, kicking at stones and looking for Indian artifacts. I hunted for crawfish in the shallows. I watched the birds—martins

The Sediment of Fishing

swooping over the water snagging insects, ducks bobbing in little flotillas out in the middle, hawks circling overhead, crows perched in the oaks along the ridges. I spied on chipmunks and squirrels, dragonflies and mayflies, turtles and frogs.

I kept darting furtive glances at my rod, of course. I believed that fishing—even stillfishing in a pond with worms—demanded skill and cleverness. Patience was no virtue. I was fishing hard the whole time.

Walden is the most famous pond in the world. A million people visit it every year. They stroll its margins, mindful of the signs that urge them to stick to the mulched pathways in the interest of erosion control. They aim for the cove at the western end, where granite markers outline the site of Henry's cabin. They drop a pebble onto the cairn and think Transcendental Thoughts. Some of them sit against the trunk of a pine tree and sketch, or write poetry, or read from a tattered paperback.

I was no pilgrim, no Thoreau devotee, no philosopher. I did not go to Walden because I'd studied a book. For me, in fact, it was the other way around: The pond directed me to the book, and I read it long before I understood that it was Profound. It was just a book about a place that I knew from sitting on its banks watching—and pretending not to watch—my rod tip.

Thoreau, I figured, was a lot like the ten-year-old me. He liked to wander around looking randomly at things, and, like me, he seemed to have plenty of time for it. He probably liked to whittle points onto the ends of sticks and take off his shoes, roll up his pant legs, and try to catch crayfish.

Yet I had the sense that he, too, was keeping a furtive eye on something else, something larger and more significant than a dragonfly or a chipmunk or a leaf. When I was ten, even though I didn't have a name for it, I knew what he was talking about. "Time," he said, "is but the stream I go a-fishing in." More than forty years ago I understood that as well as I do now.

Although Henry wasn't much of a fisherman ("always when I have done it I feel that it would have been better if I had not fished"), I excused him because, after all, in his day Walden was "not very fertile in fish." It's a kettle pond, a hole gouged out of the sandy earth by a receding glacier and filled with meltwater from the hunk of ice that broke off there. It's surrounded by pine and oak forest. Walden's waters were—and still are— remarkably clear and pure, but, like most kettle ponds, too acidic and sterile to nurture the plant and insect life necessary to support a healthy population of self-propagating trout. A century and a half ago, when Thoreau shacked up there, the only worthwhile species that lived in Walden was pickerel. From his accounts, even they were scarce.

About fifty years after Thoreau left the pond—which was fifty years before I began going there—local game wardens began stocking it with hatchery-raised trout, converting Walden into a man-made fishery. It was full of trout when I was a boy. It still is. Some of them manage to avoid eating gobs of worms impaled on hooks—or salmon eggs or cheese-flavored marshmallows or shiners or synthetic baits—and they find enough forage to survive through several seasons. Every year someone takes a six-pound brown trout from Walden.

My time at Walden Pond taught me my first lessons about trout and trout fishing. I noticed, for example, that as soon as the fish began to suck insects off the surface, they stopped eating my worms off the bottom. So when rings began to appear on the pond's skin, I tried casting dry flies toward them, and when the trout refused to eat the bushy rejects from my father's fly box, I tried other things.

It was frustrating and fascinating in ways that waiting for a fish to come along and eat my worm had never been. I found myself fishing with an unfamiliar intensity. I tried, for the first time, to think like a trout. I realized I had a lot to learn. I tried streamers and wet flies, and I stuck to it doggedly, and finally, one day, I actually caught a trout on a fly.

I knew it had been a random event. The only thing I gave myself credit for was perseverance. I still knew nothing about what went on in a trout's brain.

Nevertheless, I was transformed. I had become a fisherman, not a mere drowner of worms.

Thus was I hooked forever on fly fishing. My addiction has driven me to rivers and stillwaters and oceans all over the continent in search of trout—and striped bass, and bonefish, and salmon, and largemouths, and anything else that will eat flies.

But lately I seem to have come full circle. I've begun to sneak off to one of my neighborhood millponds with an old fly rod and a soup can full of freshly dug worms. I lob out my baited hook, prop my rod in a forked stick, and crouch there waiting for my rod tip to twitch or my bobber to jiggle. I go for reasons akin to those that lured Thoreau, and me, to Walden: "To transact some private business with the fewest obstacles." I think better when I'm squatting on the banks of my millpond, and I notice things more sharply when I'm pretending not to watch my rod tip or my bobber.

It's hard to explain to my fly-fishing friends.

The Sediment of Fishing

When I tell them that I've spent the afternoon at a weedy millpond waiting for my bobber to dance, they're likely to nod sagely and say, "Sure. It's good to get in touch with your inner self. Return to your roots. Commune with the child in you."

"Nuts," I reply, although I recognize the element of truth in what they say. "I just want a mess of bluegills for dinner. Besides, it's kind of fun."

I suppose it must seem childish for a middle-aged fly-fishing addict to start digging canfuls of worms and lugging his clunkiest old fiberglass fly rod to a tepid little pond where no trout has lived since the powdermill was built and the stream was dammed more than a century ago.

I can't persuade my fly-fishing friends to come sit with me in the shade of the willows beside my millpond on a warm summer afternoon. I've tried to entice them with quotes from Thoreau, on the theory that Transcendental philosophy might offer the kind of serious rationalization they could buy. They shrug and say it just doesn't appeal to them. It's not their kind of fishing, and anyway, they really just can't justify squandering their time that way.

What they mean, of course, is that it's my midlife crisis, not theirs, and if that's how I choose to handle it, well, there are probably more destructive ways.

But it doesn't feel like a crisis to me.

My friends didn't spend their childhoods catching horned pout from the Old Res or learning about trout on the banks of Walden. They have no memories of countless summer afternoons spent squatting on the banks of muddy little ponds waiting for the quiver, jiggle, and dart of a cork bobber. They've never grabbed a twisted old fiberglass rod off a forked stick, tightened the line, hesitated, then muttered "Now!" and hauled back, poised at that delicious instant of not knowing whether the fish on the end will come flying through the air into the bushes behind them, or if it will bend their rod double.

It's all too simple, they say. There's nothing to it. Where's the challenge? Where's the skill?

My fly-fishing friends can, simply by observing its riseform, judge the size and species of a trout and whether it's eating nymphs, emergers, duns, or spinners. In that respect, they're better fishermen than I am.

But they don't know that bluegills make a bobber twitch and bounce half a dozen times before they begin to tow it around in slow circles, that yellow perch drag it on a straight and steady line, and that a largemouth bass will yank it under so fast that it pops audibly. My fly-fishing friends know the precise moment to lift their rod when a trout takes their dry fly or nymph, but they've never learned that perch take the worm all at once while bluegills nibble, and that it's deceptively tricky to hook panfish in the lips when you're using worms.

But I shouldn't try to find complexities in something that is, in fact, simple. Expert bobber-watching requires no great skill or knowledge—just time and patience. These are commodities I had in abundance as a child. An afternoon at my millpond confirms that I haven't exhausted my supply. Now, well into middle age, I find this comforting to know.

Sure, my millpond is no Walden, never mind a Paradise Valley spring creek or northwoods smallmouth lake. The water of my millpond reminds me of the Old Res. It carries that same nostalgic, faintly septic odor in midsummer, and while I always hope that a big old bass might decide to eat my worm, it rarely happens. Most of the bluegills and crappies I catch are too small to filet, and the tiny ones can drive me crazy, filching my bait without ever taking the hook into their mouths. The hum of highway traffic from behind the hill reminds me that telephones and fax machines lurk nearby. There are always mosquitoes.

But there are dragonflies and damselflies in a hundred different neon colors, too, and they perch on my rod where I can admire them. Mother ducks lead parades of half-grown duck-lings along the edges of the lily pads. Muskrats and watersnakes carve vees across the water. Herons high-step slowly through the shallows, better fishermen than I, although I can sit as motionless as they can stand, and I don't frighten them away. Painted turtles sun themselves on the rocks. Bullfrogs grump and burp, and bluegills spat in the weeds. Swallows swoop over the water, ticking the surface here and there with their wingtips, leaving behind their own distinct riseforms.

And best of all, it doesn't require much concentration to keep an eye on my bobber, so I see it all.

There are no trout. But carp and suckers and eels live in my little millpond, and bluegills and sunfish and crappies and horned pout and white and yellow perch and bass and pickerel. Each species jiggles a bobber differently. I know I will catch plenty of fish, and I never know which kind will bite next, and I like both the knowing and the not knowing equally.

I keep my old fiberglass fly rod in the back of the hall closet. It's missing a guide, and the ancient Pfleuger reel is held on with duct tape. It amazes me that I once used it to cast dry flies. Now it's my millpond rod. With this outfit I can sling a bobber and a baited hook with just the right amount of force to get it out

The Sediment of Fishing

19

there without the worm flying off, a skill I learned as a kid after much trial and error.

The bluegills lurk around the edges of the lily pads, and I generally catch half a dozen of them right away. Sometimes I toss them all back. Sometimes I keep the saucer-sized ones for filets. When I've cleaned out the resident bluegill pod, I cut a forked stick to hold my rod, for now it's time to wait for whatever might cruise past. Now I can watch the dragonflies. I daydream. My focus on the cork grows blurry, and I can easily convince myself that the adage is correct—Allah surely does not deduct from the allotted time of man those hours spent fishing.

Maybe my friends are right after all. Maybe I go to my millpond to fool myself. Maybe bobber-watching does allow me to regress that long distance back to my childhood days on the banks of the Old Res and Walden Pond, when time was my greatest resource and when everything—including fishing—was clear and uncomplicated.

3

Panfish Are for Kids

If panfish weren't so plentiful, I'd be tempted to suggest that only kids should be allowed to catch them.

But, of course, if they weren't so plentiful, panfish wouldn't be perfect for kids.

I suspect that a lot of enthusiastic adult fishermen got that way by catching panfish when they were kids. If they started any other way, they probably didn't catch much, in which case they probably didn't become enthusiastic adult fishermen.

Some adults still fish enthusiastically for panfish. They use fine expensive tackle and clever lures and flies. They study the habits of their quarry and they practice stealth and cunning. It's no insult to panfish—or to the adults who fish for them that way—to point out that most of the time neither fancy gear nor subtle tactics are needed. Normally, panfish do not feed selectively or cautiously. They are easy to catch.

The first fish I ever caught was a bluegill the size of my hand. Since I was barely two years old at the time, and my hand was proportional to the rest of my body, this was not a large fish.

Several thousand hand-sized bluegills (and sunfish and crappies, and thumb-sized yellow perch and horned pout) later, my thoughts gradually began to turn to more exotic quarry such as trout and bass.

It took that long. For the beginning, panfish were what I wanted.

I suppose if trout or bass had been as abundant and easy to catch, they would have suited me equally well.

Although my hand has grown considerably since then, I still occasionally quest for hand-sized bluegills. But that's because I still occasionally feel like a kid and want from fishing what I wanted then: I want an absolute guarantee that I'll catch lots of fish.

Panfish are for kids of all ages.

Although I was once a young kid, I'm reluctant to rest my claim to expertise on that fact. So I asked some kids I know what makes fishing fun.

Sarah, who is nine, said, "I want to catch a lot of fish. Otherwise it's boring. I don't care if they're big and I don't care what kind they are. And I don't like to unhook them. I also like to paddle around in a canoe."

Melissa, who was nine only a few years ago but who has become more worldly since, put it this way: "I want it to be peaceful and I don't like it unless the weather's nice. And I want to catch lots of fish."

And Michael, another former nine-year-old and now on the cusp of adulthood, said this: "Back when I was a kid, all I wanted to do was catch a lot of fish. Now I like to catch a lot of fish on flies. If I can't, I guess I'll catch them some other way."

Having been a kid, and having raised three of them, I have learned some things about how kids think.

Kids are big on instant gratification. They want success, and lots of it, and they want it now. They are correspondingly bad at patience. They have short attention spans. Their minds wander. They lack focus. Their entire world is a wonder. Gathering night crawlers after dark is as much fun as catching fish with them the next day. Frogs and dragonflies and water lilies and rusty beer cans fascinate kids as much as fish do. They'd just as soon practice skipping flat stones as casting a fly.

Give them frequent short doses of fishing. Quit before it gets slow. Then help them try to catch a frog or a dragonfly. Throw some stones into the water. Pick a bouquet of lilies. See how many rusty beer cans you can hand-capture by wading the shallows. Bring the beer cans home with you and refrain from preaching about it. You won't need to.

Kids are democratic. To them, a fish is a fish regardless of its species or reputation. Two small fish are twice as good as one big one. Kids measure their success by numbers. They'd rather catch a bucketful of sunfish in an afternoon than one or two trout.

Kids are suspicious of anything that smacks of a "lesson." Adults take heed. If kids don't want to bait their own hook, don't make a big deal out of it. This is no time for a lecture. Put the worm on the hook and toss it into the water for them. When a fish bites, help them set the hook. Then unhook their catch for them. Hold it so they can touch its colors. When they're ready to try these things for themselves, they'll let you know. In the meantime, be assured that they're watching how you do it.

Kids are impatient with process. They see no sense in artfulness for its own sake. Fancy methodology does not impress them. They want results. Kids want it to be simple. Panfish are easy to catch in vast numbers using a wide variety of methods. There's no need to complicate things, although complicated methods work well, too. Kids may be quick and energetic, but they lack skill. Start them fishing with methods that don't require skill. They'll pick up the skills quickly if they want to. They'll probably want to once the fishing bug bites them.

Panfish were created especially for kids.

In New England virtually every body of fresh water contains large quantities of panfish in fascinating varieties—bluegills, sunfish, perch, shiners, horned pout, crappies, usually all sharing the same habitat. The same is more or less true of every region of the country. There are eight kinds of sunfish with names that kids love—shellcracker and redear and pumpkinseed and bream. There are black and white crappies and yellow and white perch and yellow and black and brown bullheads. It's hard to find a place where panfishing isn't good.

A panfish, more or less by definition, is anything edible that isn't a game fish. They tend to be small—pan-sized—but they fight enthusiastically. And they are beautiful, although adults sometimes need to be reminded by kids to admire the shimmering multicolored iridescence of a pumpkinseed sunfish or the infinite shades of purple and orange on a bluegill's throat.

Panfish eat everything. A worm dangled under a float near the bottom will bring bites from anything that lives in the water. Kids enjoy the suspense of not knowing what's causing their bobber to jiggle. So do adults. Grubs and crickets and small minnows work well, too. A small spinner-and-worm rig trolled behind a canoe is a fail-safe way for your daughter to catch her first fish. The same rig flipped from a light spinning outfit will reward her early casting efforts. And when she's ready to try fly casting, bluegills will gobble rubber-legged floaters anywhere beyond the tip of her rod. She'll miss a lot of strikes. That's okay. There will be plenty more.

Any handy gear will do for kids. Light tackle is best, simply because kids like to feel the tugging and slashing and circle-swimming of the small fish on the end of their line.

Adults sometimes like to make it all more complicated. But catching panfish really is that simple. Which is the way it should be for kids, no matter how old they are.

It's a good thing, I think, for an adult to try to remember what it's like to be a kid. It's even better sometimes to act like one.

4

The Perfect Fish

It was a fine May afternoon several years ago when Cliff called. "Wanna track down a rumor?" He made his voice low and conspiratorial, knowing that was the surest way to lure me away from my desk.

"A trout rumor, I presume," I said.

I heard him chuckle. "Bring your float tube. I'll pick you up in half an hour."

During the half-hour drive from my house and the ten-minute trek through the woods, all Cliff would tell me was that he'd heard about the place from a guy he ran into at the hardware store and it sounded worth checking out.

We descended a slope, broke through the underbrush, and

found ourselves on the banks of a glassy little pond nestled in the lap of the surrounding hills. "Brook trout," I thought. "Native brookies."

Cliff rigged up and paddled out quickly, and I was still sitting there rebuilding my leader when I heard him grunt. I looked up. His rod was steeply bowed. "What'd he take?" I called.

"Gray nymph, size twelve."

He released the fish with his back to me, so I couldn't judge its size. A nice one, I guessed by the bend in his rod and the time it had taken him to net it.

By the time I'd paddled out onto the pond beside Cliff, he had released another.

"What's the drill?" I asked him.

"Cast your nymph along the edge of the dropoff. Let it sink three or four feet. Then twitch it back."

"Slow or fast?"

"Slow's been working for me."

So that's what I did, and on my third cast I felt a bump, then a tug, then the heavy pull of a strong fish. I reeled up my slack, waiting for the trout to run. But it didn't. Instead it swam in stubborn circles, and when I finally strong-armed it to my net, I said to Cliff, "It's a damn bluegill."

The Perfect Fish

He nodded. "Take a look at it."

The fish was bronze and olive with a brilliant orange belly, a broad chest, and thick shoulders. It was, I guessed, nearly a foot long.

"Okay," I said, "so it's a big bluegill. A *very* big bluegill."

"That's the point," said Cliff.

"You told me this was a trout pond."

"No, I didn't. You assumed it was. I just didn't bother to correct you."

"You lied to me."

"Listen," he said. "If I'd told you we were going out for bluegills, would you've come?"

"I don't know." I shrugged. "Maybe not."

"Sorry you're here?"

I looked around. The little pond was glassy smooth, and the sun was warm, and redwing blackbirds were chittering in the bushes. "That was about the biggest bluegill I ever caught," I said.

"That was the rumor," said Cliff. "Secret pond, giant bluegills."

"I haven't actually gone bluegill fishing for years," I said. "Except with my kids. I mean, don't get me wrong. I love bluegills. But they're for cane poles and worms and bobbers.

You fish for bluegills in bare feet and a straw hat, you know? I just can't think of them as serious fish."

"Then maybe you better adjust your thinking, pal."

I was a towheaded toddler when I derricked in the first fish of my life. It was, naturally, a bluegill. I can still see in my mind's eye the sudden twitch and dart of the homemade wine-cork bobber, and I can hear my father, squatting beside me, whisper, "Wait . . . let him take it . . . okay, now! Heave back on it!" And then came the circle-swimming tug and pull, and I squealed, "I got him! I got him!" before the little fish came skimming across the surface to me.

I hauled it onto the grass and pounced on it and held it up by the leader, and as Dad snapped my picture I thought that bluegill had to be the most beautiful fish in the world, with its bright golden belly and shimmering blue-green flanks and its pugnacious snub-nosed shape.

Dad still has the yellowing old black-and-white photograph to commemorate the day a bluegill hooked me on fishing, and it's probably that photo rather than the specific memory that makes the moment seem so clear to me after half a century. I've watched a lot of cork bobbers twitch and dart since then, and

I've crouched beside three toddlers of my own, whispering, "Wait . . . wait . . . let him take it. . . ."

In my family, would-be anglers are initiated as soon as they can walk without falling down. A wine cork is split and bound to a leader and a worm is threaded onto a hook and lobbed out beside some lily pads. Then the rod—in my family, it's a fly rod—is handed to the child with the certain knowledge that sooner or later a bluegill will eat the worm and jiggle the bobber and create a fisherman.

If bluegills weren't so abundant and easy to catch, it would be easier to respect them.

Bluegills occupy a special place in my angling heart, of course. But how can you take seriously the first fish you ever caught, and, later, the first fish you caught on a fly? It's hard not to think of the bluegill as a toddler's fish. Serious fishermen just naturally move on to more serious fish and leave bluegills for the kids.

These were the thoughts I had as I drifted on Cliff's secret pond that May afternoon. "Adjust your thinking," he'd said, and as the afternoon slid into evening, and as we continued to catch those dinner-plate bluegills on light trout tackle, it became easier. They ate insect imitations, just like trout—first the nymphs that we twitched along the dropoffs, and later, after the sun had dropped behind the hills, the white-winged dry flies that we cast toward shore. They took eagerly, like the trout of my dreams, and they challenged the little two-weight outfit I was using.

And once I'd stopped comparing them with trout, I recognized their beauty. They came in myriad colors—sunflower yellow, sunset orange, midnight purple, sky blue. They weren't sleek sprinters, but they were muscular street-fighters, stubborn and powerful.

Yes, they were almost too easy to catch, and they were not especially selective or wary, and yes, we did catch them until our arms ached. And no, I knew I would not give up my trout and bass and salmon and devote the rest of my fishing life exclusively to bluegills.

But something important happened to me that afternoon, something that I realized had been missing from my fishing life for too many years: I relaxed. I fished without self-imposed goals or expectations or pressures. I knew I would catch some fish, and I knew I could make some mistakes without blowing the opportunity of the season. Once during the afternoon I stopped casting entirely. I watched a heron stalk the shallows and admired the acrobatics of the swallows as they darted and swooped over the water, and it never occurred to me that I was squandering precious fly-fishing time.

You can catch bluegills on almost any kind of live bait—worms, crickets, grasshoppers, grubs, and small shiners. They strike ultralight spinning lures readily.

But with their small mouths and their customary diet (about 85 percent insects, 10 percent crustaceans, and 5 percent baitfish), bluegills are made for a trout-weight fly rod. They take nymphs at any time: buggy patterns in sizes eight to twelve seem to work best. In calm, shaded water they rise readily to dry flies and soft-bodied bugs fished slowly with an occasional twitch.

Bluegills thrive in a wide range of water types, from cold and clear to warm and weedy, and they're now found in all of the contiguous forty-eight states. You can catch them year-round, although they're especially vulnerable during their spring spawning season, typically when the water temperature rises to about sixty-seven degrees. They build their sand-colored, saucer-shaped spawning beds in water three feet deep or less. The nests are easy to locate and logical targets for the fisherman. After the bluegills spawn, the males remain to guard the nests while the females, which generally run a bit larger, lurk nearby in deeper water.

The world-record bluegill was a four-pound twelve-ounce monster taken in Alabama in 1950. In most waters, bluegills tend to run to a certain size, and eleven- or twelve-inch "pounders" are considered big. Where you consistently catch hand-sized (or smaller) bluegills, you are unlikely to find any much larger. A spot like Cliff's secret pond, therefore, is a treasure, and worth keeping secret.

Bluegills reproduce as aggressively as they strike, and will, if unchecked by predators, overbrowse their food supply, so it's almost always a good idea to harvest them. Keeping a mess of bluegills is a good idea for another reason: Deep fried in beer batter, or rolled in cracker crumbs and sautéed in butter, bluegill filets are a gourmet's treat.

Now Cliff and I return to our secret pond two or three times a year, and we've found a few other spots where the bluegills run big and suck in dry flies after the sun leaves the water. In fact, whenever I want a relaxing day of fly fishing, I grab my trout gear and head for a bluegill pond, absolutely confident that I will catch plenty.

Now that I've adjusted my thinking, I've come to realize that the bluegill just may be the perfect fish.

5

Unofficial Trout

My favorite trout pool this side of Montana is about the size of my livingroom. If I hit it just right, I'll find four or five fish sipping insects off the surface, and if I'm lucky I'll catch two or three of them in that magical hour before dark.

They'll run from eight inches to a foot long. I'll keep one for supper and put the others back.

It takes me three-quarters of an hour to bushwhack in to my pool. The only path was made by deer. I slog through swamp and blowdown and alder tangle. Mosquitoes the size of hummingbirds lie in ambush along the entire route. There's only one place beside the pool where a fisherman can stand, and even there anything except a rollcast will snag in the alders. A careless approach rolls a ripple of alert across the surface, which sends the resident trout scooting upstream for the evening, and then there's nothing else to do except turn around and bushwhack out the way I came in.

Half the time it's dead anyway.

Objectively, it's not much of a trout pool.

Except it's mine—and, I believe, mine alone—and therefore it's special.

I could catch more and bigger trout by consulting the official list of trout waters published annually by the state. I could park my car in the officially designated parking area, launch my canoe from the official boat launch, or follow the official streamside path, and, provided I could find a place to stand between two other officially licensed trout fishermen, I could catch the trout that were officially put there for my angling pleasure.

For some reason, I haven't found much pleasure in any of that lately. In fact, increasingly I find myself thirsting for an escape from trout officialdom. I'll happily sacrifice the abundance, size, and certainty of well-publicized and generously stocked official waters for a chance at something wild and solitary.

Unofficial Trout

I'm willing to work for it. In fact, I *want* to work for it.

The little trickle that widens briefly into the aneurysm that is my favorite trout pool originates at a hillside springhole four miles from my home in eastern Massachusetts. Frigid water seeps from the rocks, wends downhill, and more or less disappears into a trackless swamp. There it is joined by a few other spring-fed rivulets. It widens as it meanders through a mosquito jungle, enters a woodland a mile from the nearest highway, and finally merges with an official trout stream.

I found it one winter on a topographic map, a thin, blue, nameless line. It's only three miles long. What I liked about it when I discovered it was the fact that no road passed over it along its entire length.

There was no place on it for a hatchery truck to stop. Therefore, it would never appear on any official list.

I figured a few trout dumped into the Official Stream might wander up into it, and I also figured that no fishermen would follow them.

I was right on both accounts. And—a bonus—I have caught enough four-inch brookies out of it to confirm my suspicion that it held natives. And on two occasions I have busted off thick-bellied browns that might've measured fifteen inches—

evidence that my little nameless trickle supports a few carry-
overs.

My private trout pool is not unique. By consulting topographic maps or following tributaries of known trout streams, I
have discovered four other nameless rills that hold trout within
a one-hour drive and half-hour bushwhack of my home.

Using the same methods, I have discovered at least a dozen
trickles that are populated only with blackflies and snakes. Gold
prospectors have to sift through a lot of worthless stuff to find
a few nuggets, too.

Discovering these rare little jewels is its own reward.
Catching trout out of them poses other challenges.

In hard-fished public waters, trout tend to be leader- and
hook-shy. They eat warily and are often hard to fool. On the
other hand, they tend to grow indifferent to wading fishermen.
They learn that the angler himself poses no threat; it's the little
piece of glitter or feather with the hook in it that they have to
watch out for.

On the trickles, it's the other way around. Trout that are not
fished over know that to survive they must eat whatever is available. Small streams rarely support abundant populations of
insects or other trout forage. A few ants or beetles may plop

into the water, mosquito larvae sometimes wiggle toward the surface, the odd mayfly or caddis or midge may hatch. Unofficial trout eat whatever they can find.

This simplifies the angler's problem. He's just as likely to raise a trout to a bushy Royal Coachman or hopper as he is to a drab, sparsely tied, hatch-imitating emerger pattern. Drifting a worm or live caddis larva on a dry-fly hook knotted to a 4X tippet is no different, really, from nymph fishing, and it's just as much fun. Unofficial trout are not selective.

But unofficial trout will spook instantly, and ask questions later, at the first hint that a predator has invaded the neighborhood.

This makes sense. All creatures, to survive, must quickly learn to identify the dangers that are peculiar to their environment. In small hard-to-find streams, where food does not come equipped with hooks, half of the survival equation is solved by eating whenever possible. Here, trout learn that feeding is not dangerous.

They understand, however, that predators abound. In small brooks, they cannot hide in ten feet of water behind a midstream boulder and know that they are safe from the jaws of a mink or the talons of an osprey or the beak of a heron. They never feel safe, so they must remain continuously alert.

To unofficial trout, a fisherman is just another predator. If they are aware of his presence, they will flee.

To catch them, therefore, the angler must mimic the other trout predators. More than once I have wasted a hellish half-hour slog through a swamp by stepping too carelessly into the water, or wearing bright-colored clothing, or splashing out a poorly thrown cast. For this kind of fishing, the stalking skills of the hunter are more important than the casting and hatch-matching techniques of the angler. One of the benefits of fishing these private places is knowing that nobody will see me when I creep through mud on hands and knees or crouch behind a tree trunk or a bush beside the water. I'm sure I look foolish.

I don't normally wear waders or hip boots when I fish these places. I don't mind getting muddy and wet, and as much as possible I try to avoid stepping into the water. I crouch on the bank and keep my silhouette broken by the streamside shrub-bery. I like to travel light for that long bushwhack in. I carry a little seven-foot fiberglass fly rod, and I stick a box of flies and a spool of tippet material into one shirt pocket and a container of insect repellent into the other. I carry nippers and forceps on a string around my neck. I wear old sneakers and blue jeans and a tan shirt. I don't feel under-equipped.

Hidden trout trickles, like their larger official counterparts, come in all shapes and designs. Some of them tumble down mountainsides, pausing here and there to form dappled rock-strewn pools. Others meander through swamp and marsh. They feature runs, riffles, pools, undercuts, and glides, just like full-sized trout rivers.

To find where the trout live in them, the angler must invest time and risk the wrath of blackflies and mosquitoes. The trickles that I have discovered do not give up their secrets willingly. The easiest way to prospect these little rills for trout is to find them rising or to spot them ghosting against the bottom. I have spent hours creeping slowly along the banks, peering into the water through my polarized glasses. I fish all the likely-looking spots carefully, and I feel fortunate if I find four or five pools or bends per mile that I can fish with the confidence that trout live there. Long stretches of water, many of which look trouty, are barren. The reason, I have concluded, is simple: Except for a few places, these little streams are not especially hospitable to trout. Few places offer the right combination of food, protection, and comfortable water temperatures for trout survival. Those that do rarely support more than a couple of fish. My favorite pool, where I know half a dozen trout live, is unusual.

Many places that may look good to a fisherman hold no trout because they lack one or more of the qualities that make them look good to fish.

Unofficial trout trickles simply cannot support a heavy population of trout. If they could, they'd be on the state's official list. They tend to be relatively sterile of aquatic insect life and they are highly sensitive to fluctuations in water volume, temperature, and oxygen content. So the trout who live in them are scattered, hard to find, wary, and short-lived—which only makes catching one of them a greater triumph.

Although unofficial trout will sometimes move into flats and riffles to gluttonize on a hatch, most commonly they rest their bellies on the bottom of the deepest and darkest water available to them, where they can feel relatively safe from predators. I look for undercut banks where the stream bends, gouged-out pools beneath waterfalls, springholes, and beaver ponds. The very best way to catch them is on a worm and fly rod. But even though these fish hang near the bottom, they tend to keep an eye cocked toward the surface, and they will dart up with startling quickness to gobble a dry fly.

Exploring unofficial trout streams isn't for everybody. If you consider an afternoon of slogging through mud, slapping mosquitoes, tangling lines, and catching no fish a waste of time, you're better off following your state's official trout guidelines.

But if you thirst for solitude, if you treasure the illusion that your footprint is the only human one ever made in the mud, if you ache to catch a ten-inch trout that was not officially planted there by the government for your angling enjoyment, get yourself a topographic map and go prospecting.

You'll have to sweat and bleed for your trout. I, for one, prefer it that way.

II

Mysteries and Revelations

Angling can be said to be so like the mathematics that it can never be fully learnt.

—Izaak Walton, *The Compleat Angler*

6

Trout Hunting

The PMDs came off at eleven, just the way I'd heard they would, and I wasted an hour casting dun imitations to trout that were eating emergers before I figured it out, and another hour finding a pattern and method of presentation that caught me my very first Western spring creek brown trout.

The other anglers up- and downstream from me had bends in their rods throughout the hatch. That was okay. Despite all my years of casting flies for trout back East, I had expected this spring creek deal to be different. I had come here seeking smart trout that would challenge me with complicated problems, unforgiving trout that would not take pity on me if I made mistakes, large trout that would reward me with their beauty and their energy if I finally factored all the variables correctly and got one to eat my fly.

If I'd wanted it to be easy, I would've stayed home. I'd refused to ask the other fishermen for their secrets. I wanted to figure it out for myself.

That brown trout measured fourteen inches against the markings on my rod. An average trout for that spring creek, but special because it was my first, and because I had taken it on its own terms, and because the process had taught me something.

After I released that first one, I caught two or three more before the hatch petered out. The trout stopped rising. And one by one, the other anglers reeled in and sloshed to shore. I did the same.

They had gathered by their cars parked in the shade of the big cottonwoods. They were debating leader formulas and emerger patterns and *inermis* vs. *infrequens* while they stowed their vests in the trunk, tugged off their waders, and and broke down their rods.

What are these guys doing? I thought. I saw them catch a lot of trout while I was struggling to figure it out. What else do they know that I don't? This long Montana summer day was only half gone, yet they were turning their backs on the most beautiful trout stream in the world. So far I had resisted asking anybody anything. But I wasn't proud.

"Quitting already?" I said to one older gentleman who was carefully sliding a beautiful cane rod into its case.

"It's dead time," he said. "I'm heading up to Livingston for lunch. Some of the guys'll take naps. Nothing'll happen until the sulphurs come off, and that won't be for a few hours."

"Nothing?"

He smiled indulgently. Obviously he'd been here before and knew the drill. "Well," he said, "if you want to dredge nymphs with strike indicators . . ."

I didn't want to dredge nymphs with strike indicators. I wanted to cast dry flies. Somehow strike indicators on a spring creek struck me as sacrilege.

On the other hand, I had no intention of wasting my precious afternoon here. I had waited too long, come too far.

I salvaged a soupy Hershey bar and a warm can of Coke from my car and took my standard trout-fishing lunch to a bench overlooking Betty's Riffle. The midday August sun beat down relentlessly from a cloudless Montana sky. A freshening downstream breeze brought relief from the dry heat.

I watched the water, and, as the gentleman had predicted, I saw no rising trout. Warblers flitted in the willows. Grasshoppers buzzed and hopped around in the grass. Ants crawled on my waders. A neon-blue dragonfly perched on my knee.

I swiveled my head around, tearing my eyes from the stream to relish the beauty of the place. Snow dribbled from the jagged peaks of the green and purple Absarokas. From where I sat, the only signs of humanity were the rustic corral and shed, the Angler's Hut, and a couple of cars crouching in the shade of the cottonwoods. I thought of my Eastern trout streams—mobbed during the short spring season, sluggish and overheated and fishless in August.

Now here I was, in Montana's Paradise Valley. Paradise!

And I had the whole creek to myself.

I returned my gaze to the stream. The currents braided and swirled over the weedbeds, and I remembered how I had lengthened my tippet and adjusted my position to get a drag-free drift over that first trout, the one that had finally eaten my PMD emerger, and I wondered if I'd catch another when the sulphurs came off. I'd heard that when spring creek trout were rising to sulphurs they were harder to fool than when they were gluttonizing on PMDs. . . .

What was that? Against the far bank, a disturbance registered in the periphery of my vision. Hardly a disturbance.

Something out of place. An anomaly. I focused on the spot. It was no more than six inches from the bank, in the shade, directly under a tuft of grass.

A minute later I saw it again. I was disappointed. It looked as if a pebble had fallen into the water. The tiny rings widened and were quickly blotted by the gentle currents. It was hardly the businesslike boil of a feeding trout that I'd been hoping for.

But it happened a third time, in precisely the same place, and I reasoned that it was unlikely three pebbles would decide to leap into the water in that one spot.

Besides, the disturbance appeared to come from below the surface, not from above.

So I put down my Coke can, picked up my rod, and waded slowly into the stream. I savored the quick chill of the water around my legs. This was where I belonged, hatch or no hatch.

The pebble-rise came again, and from my position in midstream I was able to make out the shadowy shape of a large trout. Its flank brushed against the bank, and it hung there suspended and motionless and slightly atilt, so that its nose almost touched the surface, directly under the tuft of grass.

Aha!

When it rose the next time, I saw it all. It wasn't much of a performance. The trout simply lifted its nose so that it pricked the water, opened its mouth, and took in something invisible that had been drifting flush with the surface.

What? I wondered. What was it eating? Spinners, perhaps. The riseform suggested the familiar unhurried way trout sip inert insects, or midge pupae, drifting suspended in the surface film.

Or . . . ants. They'd been crawling all over my waders.

From where I stood midstream, I bent close to the water. Nothing whatsoever was floating past my waders. No spinners, no midge pupae, no ants.

On the other hand, it was unlikely I'd see ants in the middle of the stream. They'd be near the banks, falling or being blown onto the water.

Ants, then. I tied a No. 20 black fur ant to my 6X tippet, waded carefully until I stood upstream and to the side of the trout, false-cast sidearm to keep the shadow of the line away from the fish, then dropped the ant two feet upstream of the tuft of grass.

It drifted past him, less than four inches from where he lay. I could see it clearly—my ant, floating without drag, and the trout, ignoring it as it went past him.

I moved a step closer to the bank and cast again, a miniature reach cast. I mended extra slack into my leader, and this time my fake ant floated directly toward his nose. I watched the trout, saw a quiver in his fins, saw his nose lift so that it barely protruded through the surface film, and I saw his mouth open to intercept my ant.

Of course, seeing it all made it impossible for me to wait until he turned and closed his mouth on my fly. I reacted with all the subtlety and patience of a teenager in heat and jerked my fly from that trout's mouth.

When I'd stopped shaking and looked again, the trout was gone.

But, I figured, where there was one there might be another. I took a couple of steps downstream, focusing through my polarized glasses at the one-foot band of water that flowed in the shade directly against the bank, and I quickly spotted another little bulge on the water. This trout lay in a tiny eddy behind a grass hummock, and it took me a dozen casts before my ant floated directly onto his nose. When it did, he sipped it in confidently, and this time I expected it and murmured "Slow down, dummy" to myself before lifting my rod and feeling the sagging tug of my hook penetrating the trout's jaw.

I netted, admired, and released him, mumbled "Aha" a few times, and glanced around. I still had that section of the creek all to myself. Nobody had witnessed my feat. Sure. It was "dead" time. Everyone was off to Livingston for lunch or napping in the shade. At first I was disappointed. I had, I thought, done something wonderful, and I deserved applause.

Then I allowed myself a small self-satisfied smile. What could be better, I thought, than having this heavenly spring creek all to myself and marching along plucking trout from against the banks?

And that's precisely how it happened. I went trout hunting, and I found them lurking under tufts of grass and behind eddies. They hid under the mossbeds on the upstream side of deadfalls, poking up their noses in the half-inch of water that flowed along the edge of the matted weed. Their giveaway riseforms were so subtle that if I hadn't known what to look for I would've missed them. They refused any fly that failed to float drag-free and directly onto their noses. The careless flash of a fly line overhead or the waving of my rod spooked some of them, and I learned to cast cautiously and wade stealthily.

But they rewarded every careful stalk and perfect presentation with a slow but absolutely positive take, and in the next hour or so I caught several trout before one took me under a deadfall and broke me off.

I started to tie on another ant when my personal bugaboo—an overly inquisitive imagination—got the best of me. Were these trout really feeding selectively on No. 20 black ants? Could I have been that smart—or lucky—to have figured it out on my first try?

I had caught trout steadily for an hour. I could afford not to catch some for a while. So I tied on one of the PMD dun imitations that the fish had stoutly refused to eat during the morning hatch, drifted it over the next bank sipper I located, and he ate it. Another "aha."

I tried a beetle and caught a trout. I busted one off on a spinner, another on a cricket. I caught one on a parachute Adams, and another, for Heaven's sake, on a No. 16 Royal Wulff.

By then I thought I understood. These midday bank sippers were surface-feeding scavengers. They found a shady protected lie close to the bank or under the moss where they felt safe from predators, and they sucked in anything edible that they could reach without moving. They were agonizingly selective to presentation. But they were absolutely opportunistic when it came to pattern.

It was, of course, a valuable lesson, and in the dozen years since that afternoon on that Paradise Valley spring creek, I've successfully applied it on other trout streams East and West when I've found no hatch in progress. On the Bighorn and the Henrys Fork, the Madison and the Missouri, on Eastern limestoners and tailwaters—in fact, on virtually all trout streams large and small everywhere—I go hunting for subtle risers against shaded banks during the "dead" times between hatches. Rarely have I failed to find at least a few scavenging sippers.

It's become, in fact, a kind of specialty for me. I like to track them down, to spot them when they think they can't be spotted, to stalk them from upstream without spooking them, to factor in current and wind to achieve a drag-free float, to make that one perfect cast that brings a trout to my fly.

I'll happily spend an hour stalking and casting to a single bank sipper even when there are other less difficult fish feeding around me. These trout, I've learned, tend to be big and smart. Fooling them with dry flies gives me the ultimate trout-fishing satisfaction.

The sun was low in the sky by the time I returned to the bench at Betty's Riffle. I was sipping another warm Coke and gazing at the water when the gentleman from the parking lot came along. He sat beside me and said, "So did you try the nymph and strike indicator?"

"Didn't bother," I answered, nudging my rod behind my leg so he couldn't see the Royal Wulff that was still tied to my leader. "I'm not big on that."

He opened his flybox on his lap, plucked out a small yellowish fly, and began to tie it onto his leader. "Well, not to worry," he said. "Sulphurs'll be coming off soon, and we can get back to fishing."

7

The Fish of a Thousand Casts

My father fished for Atlantic salmon in Newfoundland and New Brunswick with Lee Wulff in the 1940s and '50s. When I was growing up and learning to love fishing, Dad would feed my enthusiasm with salmon stories. "When I first got there," he'd say, "I saw these huge brook trout in the river. I caught a couple, four- and five-pounders, and I thought it was heaven. Lee laughed and said, 'Wait till you catch a salmon.' Well, pretty soon I hooked one, and he began leaping all over the pool, this beautiful, powerful, silvery fish, and I forgot all about the trout."

When Dad talked about salmon, I'd nod and shrug and admit that it sounded like fun.

"You owe it to yourself," he'd always insist. "You've got to go salmon fishing."

And the older I got, the more insistent he became. "Go, while you still can," he'd say. But I knew it wasn't the way he remembered it anymore. I knew there weren't as many salmon as there had been forty years ago when Dad fished for them.

I knew you could expect to fish for two weeks without hooking an Atlantic salmon. I knew that you did not go salmon fishing with any particular expectation. I knew that Atlantics are called "the fish of a thousand casts" as a conservatively accurate measure of the investment required to hook one. I knew you could never predict which of those casts would bring a strike, or whether you might make two thousand casts before you earned the right to hook two fish.

I knew that on their single-minded spawning runs, salmon do not eat. But they sometimes strike at a fly for reasons that they have not divulged to us: aggression, possibly, or territoriality, or general irritability. Perhaps the feeding response is so imprinted in their brains that, like human potato-chip munchers, they sometimes eat automatically even when they're not hungry.

I knew that Atlantic salmon could be caught on the fly rod, although mostly they're not. They hunker at the bottom of a pool while a thousand flies drift over their noses, and then, inexplicably, they might rise to strike the one-thousand-and-first.

I knew that salmon fishermen argue over fly patterns—dark or bright, sparse or full, small or large. It is unclear if the salmon care, but fishermen surely do. Many of them still favor the old patterns that have been around for a hundred years. Although new fly patterns appear continually, they are mostly minor variations of older ones. Classic Atlantic salmon flies imitate nothing in particular. Instead they are elaborate and artful, on the theory, perhaps, that salmon might want to possess them out of admiration for their beauty, or that such a worthy fish deserves an elegant fly.

The only secrets in Atlantic salmon fishing belong to the salmon. The fishermen know the pools where the fish are resting. They know that their choice of fly is mostly whimsy. They begin casting at the top of the pool, a forty-five-degree across-and-down cast. They swing the fly through the current, take two steps, and repeat the cast until they arrive at the tail of the pool. Then they move back to the top, wait for the other anglers to two-step along, switch to a different pattern, and they do it again. And they do this all day, dawn to dark, through four or five pools each day, and they do it again the next day, and if they do it for a week they might catch several salmon. Or they may never get a strike.

I knew all these things, and, in spite of my father's stories, they did not truly excite me or give me confidence. But I also knew I had to go Atlantic salmon fishing while it was still possible—in my lifetime, and in the lifetime of the species. It wasn't that I owed it to myself. But I felt that I owed it to Dad.

Three fly-fishing fanatics. More than a century of combined fishing experience all over North America. Enough equipment among us to stock a good-sized fly shop. There are few trout rivers the three of us haven't fished together, and there are none of any significance that at least one of us hasn't tried. We've caught permit and tarpon and bonefish in Belize and Mexico and the Bahamas. We've caught Pacific salmon in Alaska and giant brook trout in Labrador. We've caught steelhead and shad, bass and pike, stripers and bluefish, crappies and bluegills.

But none of us had ever even tried to catch an Atlantic salmon.

Bill Rohrbacher is a trout and Pacific salmon guide by trade and a West Coast steelhead fisherman by addiction. "If I can catch steelhead," he said, "—and do not doubt, I can catch steelhead—then I can catch an Atlantic salmon. Anadromous fish. Sex-crazed. Not eating. Same deal. Same tactics. I can catch one."

Andy Gill is a psychiatrist, with his own peculiar obsessional delusion: He will cast flies for any fish anywhere anytime with the unwavering conviction that his abnormal perseverance and vast skill will ultimately reward him. Fish generally reinforce this delusion.

I'm less skillful and less fanatical than Andy and Bill. I like to spend a lot of my time on the water looking, studying, daydreaming, thinking up stories. I am, by nature, a trout fisherman. Give me feeding fish, selective and spooky and smart. Make it a problem and assure me that it has a solution, however complex, and I will gladly make one thousand casts, although I'd rather spend a lot of time scheming how to make one perfect cast.

But this salmon fishing presented mysteries, not problems. It struck me as random rather than logical. It required faith and bull-headed tenacity. I wondered if I had the temperament for it. I didn't want to admit it. But Atlantic salmon fishing sounded monotonous.

No. Boring.

We did our homework, and we chose the Margaree River on Cape Breton Island, Nova Scotia. The Margaree is one of the few significant salmon rivers whose pools are all open to the public and where a guide is not required. We could explore it and confront its mysteries ourselves.

We were attracted to the Margaree, too, because on this river fishermen are not allowed to kill the salmon they catch. Only grilse may be killed. This policy, perhaps, is responsible for the high percentage of large fish in the river.

The Margaree is small and accessible and especially beautiful in October, and we knew, although we didn't discuss it, that even if we caught no fish, we would be rewarded.

We left Boston at eight on Friday night. Andy instantly fell asleep in the back seat. Bill, younger than me by a decade, drove. He would, he insisted, drive the entire distance. "You relax, Grandfather," he told me, "and leave the driving to Bubba."

"Then I'll stay awake and talk to you," I answered, "so that you will stay awake and not destroy us on a bridge abutment before we can catch a salmon."

We filled thermoses with coffee at each gas-and-pee stop, and Bill and I reminded each other of trout we had caught in

The Fish of a Thousand Casts

Montana and Oregon and the flies we had caught them on and the time my cast had gone awry and my fly had sunk over the barb into Bill's bare chest. He had refused to let me remove the hook. Instead, he wore that fly for the rest of the day and showed it to everyone we encountered. "See what my grandfather has done to me," he would tell them.

"He's afraid it'll hurt if I pull it out," I would counter.

We worried about running out of gas toward the northern end of the Maine Turnpike, where the land is named after map quadrants because nobody lives there, and we reached Houlton around two in the morning. The customs official glanced at Andy's comatose body sprawled under the blanket. "Is he alive?" he asked.

"I don't know," I said. "But he has been snoring."

"And where are you boys headed?"

"The Margaree."

"Fishing, eh?"

"Yes."

"I should detain you because I am jealous," he said. "My son is there now. He took my good fly rod with him." He waved us through. "Good luck, eh?"

Over the border in the darkest time of the night, Andy's old Blazer chugged over the narrow Canadian roads. A soft rain fell steadily. Bill and I drank coffee and talked on. I offered to drive. "No, Grandfather," he said. "I'm in a groove."

"Don't fall asleep."

"I can drive in my sleep," he said.

We had not even come halfway. The roadsigns in kilometers made the distances seem impossibly long. But the metric speed limit was ninety, and that seemed to get us there faster.

Bill and I drank coffee and tried to remember which year had been the first one the Pale Morning Duns did not hatch on the Bighorn and exactly how long the trout was that I had caught at Lake of the Dunes and the day he had won the Ugly Fly Contest on our secret spring creek. He reminded me of the time I had refused to get up at four in the morning to fish with him and the other time when I was rowing his boat and his fly rod fell into the river.

Andy snored in the back seat.

"The young doctor in back," observed Bill, "will be bright-eyed and bushy-tailed when we get there. He'll want to go fishing."

"I'll want to sleep," I said.

"We'll all go fishing," said Bill. "We didn't come all this way to sleep."

"It'll be hard to go fishing with no sleep," I said. "It won't be fun."

"Did we come here to have fun," he said, "or to fish?"

We were traveling due east, and by the time we passed from New Brunswick into Nova Scotia, the misty sky ahead of us had turned pewter and we could see the blurry golds and scarlets washed over the autumnal countryside like a watercolor painted on wet paper. The roads narrowed, and through every valley ran a river, and there were small villages with Scottish names and white-spired churches and cattle grazing on pastures without fences. We stopped at an Irving station to empty ourselves of the old coffee and refill our mugs with fresh, and from the back seat Andy stirred and mumbled, "Are we there?"

"Oh, he'll be a ball of fire on the river," I said.

"So will we, Grandfather," said Bill.

"Andy," I said, "you'll do the cooking tonight while Bubba and I sip whiskey and rest our tired old butts."

"I will," said Andy. "I'll make us steak and fried potatoes and baked beans. But this afternoon I'll catch a salmon."

We arrived at our cabin at noon. Bill had driven for sixteen straight hours. I had stayed awake the whole time. Andy had slept all but the last three hours of it.

We had driven 850 miles through the night and half a day for our rendezvous with the salmon at the Margaree. The salmon had swum a thousand miles through the Atlantic Ocean to meet us there.

That afternoon the three of us bought licenses, assembled our gear, and headed for the river. Andy strode purposefully into the pool and began to make long graceful casts. Bill and I squatted on the riverbank, lit cigarettes, and watched. Bill read the pool to me. "If salmon are like steelhead, they'll lie in a slot like that one," he said, pointing. "I'd like to see more current," he added. "The river looks low."

We fished through the afternoon, investing our first hundred or so casts. My mind kept wandering to the steak and fried potatoes and beans that Andy would cook and the bed where I would, finally, sleep.

That night Ed Taylor came to our cabin. Ed is a local guide. We had arranged to have him show us the river for the first couple of days. We offered him a drink. "I don't mind," he said, a smile crinkling his weathered face.

The Margaree needed rain, he said. The dark salmon were sulking in the pools. Many, still silver, were waiting in the estuary for a "freshet" to bring more water into the river. Fishing had been slow.

"What's slow?" we wanted to know.

Ed shrugged. One Margaree regular had gone a week before his first hookup. Another had been on the river for eleven days with no strikes. But a few grilse had been taken. And there were fish in the pools. Ed knew which pools and where the salmon were lying in them.

"No guarantees, eh?" he said. "But you never know with salmon. Anyhow, I'll keep coffee going and make you a good hot shore lunch. How's steak and chili sound?"

It sounded good. I figured Ed's lunch would be the highlight of the day.

You never know with salmon. On our first run through our first pool of our first full day on the river, my old-fashioned little yellow featherwing wet fly stopped halfway through its swing, and I saw the boil and felt the tug and then the surge, and then the salmon leaped, bright silvery in the morning sun against the gold of the streamside maples. My first thought when I saw that fish arced over the water was that Dad would be happy when I told him about it.

Ed measured him—thirty inches, about ten pounds, not a big salmon by Margaree standards—before we released him. "Well, now," he said, grinning. "A good start, eh?"

We fished three other pools that day but had no more strikes.

The next day it rained. Ed kept squinting toward the mountains and shaking his head. "Enough to get us wet," he said. "But not enough to bring up the river." No strikes.

On the third day it snowed. Andy caught a grilse on a dead-drifted dry fly on our last run through the last pool of the day.

In the morning of the fourth day ice formed in our guides. A brittle sun shone all day. No strikes.

On the fifth day, Bill announced it was time to get serious. The fish were sulking on the bottom and needed some stirring up. So he cast a sink-tip line and a large flashy marabou streamer on his nine-weight rod. "Steelhead tactics," he shrugged. And he caught two salmon within ten minutes of each other from the same section of the same pool, thereby confirming his belief that salmon are as perverse and powerful and beautiful and altogether as worthy as steelhead.

Andy immediately switched to a sink-tip and a big black Woolly Bugger. I had already caught my salmon. I continued to cast a variety of little featherwings on a floating line.

The Fish of a Thousand Casts

Andy got his salmon on his last cast in the last pool on our last day, an enormous forty-two-inch fish that weighed, we calculated, twenty-seven pounds. Andy guessed that he was well into his second set of one thousand casts when it happened.

Meanwhile, I made the rest of my one thousand casts and most of my second thousand, too, and never had another strike. I did not become bored. I remembered the feel of that tug and surge and the picture of that silver arc over the river. It could, I now knew, happen again, any time. If not this year, maybe next. I already had an investment in another salmon.

8

The Gulper Rules

The first time I cast to a Hebgen Lake gulper, I dropped my fly dead center in the widening rings of the big trout's riseform. Bullseye, I thought, glancing smugly at Bob Lamm, who was paddling along beside me in his float tube.

"Lousy cast," he said.

"Are you kidding?" I said. "That happened to be a perfect cast."

He chuckled. "Not if you want to catch that fish. Slow down and think about it."

I didn't want to think. I wanted to fish. Rings pocked the glassy skin of the lake all around us. Several trout swirled within a thirty-foot cast of our tubes, poking up their noses to slurp in the freshly hatched *callibaetis* duns that were trying to dry their wings in the moist early-morning air.

They were obviously worthy trout. Seventeen to twenty inches, Bob had promised, strong and well fed. And they were gobbling mayflies off the surface. Who could think?

But this was my debut at gulper fishing, and Bob was an old hand at it, so I tried. After a minute, I said, "Okay. I get it. They're cruising."

"Right," said Bob. "Worst place to cast is into the rings. You can't always tell where they're going. But it's for dang sure that the one place they ain't gonna be is where they just were. See, it's just the opposite of stream fishing. In moving water, the fish hold a lie and wait for the food to come floating to them. In still water, the bugs stay put, so the fish've gotta go get 'em. Rule Number Two in gulperin': Take your best guess, and lead your trout."

"What's Rule Number One?"

"You've gotta be in the right place at the right time. I thought that was self-evident."

"I guess it is," I said.

A minute later Bob pointed with his rod. "There. That one's really gulpin'. Try him."

The Gulper Rules

The fish was coming fast at eleven o'clock, moving straight toward me. Every three or four feet he lifted his head, cut a wake across the water, and sucked in several bugs.

I imagined that I could hear him gulp.

Piece of cake.

I dropped my No. 18 parachute Adams directly in his path and held my breath. I stared at its smoke-colored wing with one eye and watched the trout close the distance with the other. A collision course.

"Eat!" I whispered.

Of course, he veered away a scant yard before he arrived at my fly.

"Quick," whispered Bob. "Again!"

I lifted, false cast once, laid it out there.

But the fish had gone down.

"Guess I spooked him," I said.

"Doubt it. He's a trout, that's all. He goes where he wants."

Which, I was to learn, is Gulper Rule Number Three.

We had launched our float tubes before daybreak. Morning mist hovered over Hebgen, shrouding the shoreline and the snow-topped peaks beyond. It was August in Montana, and soon enough the sun would burn off the mist, but in the dawn's half-light the air was still cool and liquid. The water's surface lay as flat and dark as carbon paper. It was eerie and silent and beautiful, and suspended out there half in and half out of the water, neither of us cared to violate the tranquility of the place by talking. So we paddled in comfortable and companionable silence across the narrow Madison Arm of the lake toward the steeply banked north shore. That's where the rainbows would come out to play, Bob had said.

The lake was scummy with spent Trico spinners, but only an occasional isolated swirl disturbed its surface. "Do we chase them?" I asked Bob.

He shook his head. "They're just foolin' around until the *callibaetis* come off. Sometimes they get up and really munch those Tricos, but mostly before it's light enough to fish for 'em. That little box of Adams parachutes is all you need for gulpers."

By the time we had finned halfway across the lake, a scattering of speckled duns had begun to pop to the surface. A few trout rose, more duns appeared, and the hatch was under way. Soon I could count a dozen rising trout within casting distance of my float tube. I'd waited a long time for a crack at these Hebgen Lake gulpers. I could wait no longer.

That's when I began to strip line off my reel and aimed for the bullseye. And that's when I learned the three rules of gulper fishing.

We were there and the trout were gulping. We'd already obeyed Rule Number One. So I attempted to apply rules Two and Three. An occasional fish exhibited classic "gulping" behavior, waking across the surface for several bites, dropping down briefly, then coming up to gluttonize again. Those trout, I saw, moved erratically. Some of them plowed steadily in a straight line before dropping out of sight. Some zigzagged, some took sharp right-angle turns, some moved in a long curve.

Most of the trout, however, did not "gulp." They rose to the surface, ate once or twice, then descended, only to rise again six to ten feet away.

There were always plenty of fish to cast to, and I tried them all. I'd spot a rising trout, guess his route, cast ahead of him, and wait, tense and poised. It was exhilarating. It was heart-stopping. It didn't take me long to understand that gulper fishing was addictive.

It was also futile. Invariably my target trout chose a route other than the one I'd chosen for him and rose somewhere other than where my fly sat. In an hour I never raised a single fish.

By then Bob had taken two fat rainbows. Eighteen inches, I estimated.

"Should I change flies?" I finally said to him.

"I'm using the same one you are."

"Maybe I should go down to 6X."

"I'm using 4X, myself."

"I'm going to watch you."

I paddled over and treaded water beside him. A trout swirled forty feet from him at two o'clock. He false cast once and dropped his fly thirty feet away at three o'clock.

"Why'd you cast there?"

"That's where he's headed," he grunted, straining forward in his tube. A black snout lifted and Bob's fly disappeared. "There. See?"

"Of course I see," I muttered.

He played, netted, and gently released the rainbow, a triplet of his previous two. He blew on his fly and smiled at me.

"Okay," I said. "So there's a trick to it."

He shrugged. "Not really. Experience, that's all. I'm not sure I can explain it, but I've been doing this for a while. I can tell where they're headed. Oh, not every time. They don't always go straight. Like I say, they're trout, after all. Grant 'em a little free will. But you watch their riseforms closely and you'll get it. I couldn't tell you exactly what I see, but there's a head and a tail and a curve to their body and a movement to their fins and a shape to their swirl, and it all somehow computes. All I can tell you is, it's more than guessing and less than knowing."

"Zen and the art of gulper fishing," I mumbled.

"Exactly!" said Bob.

When I finally got it, it did feel like Zen, or something equally mysterious. I flicked my fly to the left and a little beyond the swirl of one particular trout, and for no reason that I could explain I was absolutely confident I had it right. And I was not at all surprised when his nose lifted and his mouth clamped down on my little Adams.

Around midmorning the activity began to abate, so we paddled back across the lake to the shallower southern shore. There we found brown trout gulping among the reeds. Like the rainbows, the browns averaged seventeen or eighteen inches. Like the rainbows, too, they exercised plenty of free will, and it required all of my Zen powers to get it right—to "see" their route—and intercept a few of them.

Before the wind came up—as it does every day in Montana—to blow the bait and the float tubes off the water, I got it wrong plenty of times, too. Rule Number Three. Trout are trout, after all. If they weren't, who'd bother trying so hard to catch them?

Since that magical August morning with Bob several years ago, I've paddled my float tube out onto Hebgen Lake many times. I've found that following Rule Number One—being there at the right time—requires only enough self-discipline to wake up in the dark. The prospect of gulper fishing gives me remarkable self-discipline. The *callibaetis* hatch comes off every August morning, as dependable as the sunrise. It lasts for more than a month, and until the wind starts blowing, the trout cruise the surface to eat the duns. My main problem in catching them is still figuring out where they're going to rise next. Quick, accurate casting and a delicate presentation help, and aggressively chasing a riser gives more opportunities.

Otherwise it's not hard. Drag, the bane of stream fishermen, is no problem on still water. Gulpers feed confidently. They are not particularly leader-shy—I usually use 4X—nor do they seem wary of a fisherman in a tube, so long-distance casting is rarely called for. I have not found gulpers particularly selective to fly pattern. If the good old Adams isn't the perfect *callibaetis* imitation, it's close enough for Hebgen gulpers. Although I prefer the parachute style, I've had good success with thorax, no-hackle, and the old-fashioned Catskill ties.

My gulper rod is a nine-foot, high-modulus graphite for a four-weight line. I believe that the long rod allows me to pick up and cast quickly to a moving fish. I'm sure I could get by with a heavier rod, but I don't need it. Wind is not a factor. If there's wind, the fish don't feed anyway.

I love the maneuverability and low profile of the float tube, and the one-on-one simplicity of it seems to fit the spirit of gulper fishing. Some fishermen chase gulpers from canoes or boats equipped with electric motors. Others like to stalk them by wading the shallows. The choice, really, is personal. The three Gulper Rules must be heeded regardless.

Hebgen Lake is rightfully famous for its gulper fishing. But it's not the only place to go, which is fortunate. I'm too addicted to gulpering to be satiated by my annual two-week Montana trek. I've cast dry flies to gulping trout on ponds and lakes and reservoirs in many parts of North America. I've found trout eating midges off the surface of Cape Cod kettle ponds at dawn, in the spring and again in the fall. These trout behave exactly the way their larger Hebgen Lake cousins behave, and they will fall for a well-cast Griffith's Gnat or, even more deadly (but perhaps not quite as much fun), a midge pupa twitched slowly across their path.

At the opposite end of the scale are the giant brookies in Labrador's Minipi area, which like to gluttonize on the huge brown and green drakes that hatch on those wilderness lakes during the brief summer season, and will readily gobble down almost any big dry fly that appears in their path.

But there are many stillwaters where trout are abundant and grow large yet rarely feed off the top. I have concluded that trout will come to the surface to gulp only if a significant portion of their habitual diet consists of hatching aquatic insects. All things being equal, trout prefer to feed beneath the surface. A lake or pond with lavish populations of leeches, baitfish, scuds, crayfish, or nymphs is unlikely to offer reliable gulper fishing.

Gulping, in other words, is an acquired trout behavior, an adaptation to an environmental condition. Hebgen Lake is shallow and weedy and rich in insect life. When the *callibaetis* are hatching, they're the best meal available. Cape Cod ponds tend to be sterile. Hatching midges are often the only food available to trout. And, aside from the giant mayflies, the lakes of

Labrador do not provide trout with rich and varied forage. They eat what's most readily available. When they've got hatching mayflies, cruising at the surface is their most efficient feeding behavior.

And for the angler who knows the rules, casting dry flies into their path is the most efficient way to catch them.

9

Turkey Bones

When Keith Wegener called and said "Be here at four," I knew better than to ask why. If I had, he would've said, "Okay, don't," and then hung up on me, and I would've had to call him back.

A Wegener summons in April means that the ice has gone out of Sebago and the landlocks are chasing smelt around the mouth of the Songo. In October, it means that flights of woodcock have dropped into the Stick Farm and the Hippie House and his other alder covers. In December, "be here" means that the weatherman has promised one of those winter storms that gets flocks of eiders and old squaws flying over Casco Bay.

When Keith called in July, I figured it meant he'd found some stripers.

"A.M. or P.M.?" I said, the only response that would forestall a hangup.

"P.M."

"That's a relief."

"Tide," he elaborated, and hung up.

He'd already untrailered and loaded his boat at the landing when I got there. I grabbed my gear from the back seat and went down to the water's edge. I frowned and pretended to look around. "Where's the boat?"

Keith is the only man I know who does his fishing from a camouflaged duck boat. He claims that it makes him invisible.

He grinned quickly, then jerked his head at the ten-weight fly rod I was carrying. "See you brung your toy rod."

"I can land a keeper on this," I said.

"Well," he drawled, "I surely hope you can."

I first met the striper forty-odd years ago. Linesides were abundant back then, and my father liked to troll big surface plugs off the stern of my Uncle Woober's lobster boat in the mouth of the Piscataqua River near Portsmouth, New Hampshire. Those bass ran large—twenty and thirty pounds— too big and strong, according to the men, for a second-grader to haul in. They crashed those plugs, and sometimes whole schools of them churned the water chasing bait. I vowed that when I was big enough, I was going to catch stripers myself.

But, of course, something happened, and Dad put away his boat rods and his surf rods and his boxes of scarred wooden plugs, and my rich fishing childhood centered around bluegills and pickerel and largemouth bass and trout. I fished with worms and shiners. I learned bait-casting. But once I started using a fly rod, I never put it down.

So when the stripers started coming back a few years ago, it was natural that I'd fish for them with flies. I never felt particularly handicapped. Whenever I was able to find fish, I generally could catch some on Deceivers or poppers, and the striped bass and I hooked each other on the fly rod. I discovered that stripers could be both aggressive and selective. Some days they crashed poppers like largemouths. Other days they sucked in small baitfish imitations like nymphing trout. They fought harder, pound for pound, than any freshwater game fish.

Time on the water is always the best teacher. I believe that I can decipher a trout river in a day or two. But several years is not enough time to learn the Atlantic Ocean. So I depend on the kindness of strangers and friends like Keith Wegener to find stripers for me. Show me some fish, I tell them, and I will catch them.

Keith and I climbed into his duck boat, and he steered it through the marsh and up a meandering tidal creek. We made jokes about being invisible.

Finally, unable to restrain myself any longer, I said, "So you found a hot spot for stripers, huh?"

"Ayuh."

"Big ones?"

"Mebbe."

"Keepers?"

Apparently exhausted from the conversation, he just shrugged, which I took for an affirmative.

We followed the creek through several miles of marsh before Keith turned the boat around and cut the motor to trolling speed. He pointed at the shoreline, where the outgoing tide swirled around rocks and cut deep holes against the marsh grass. I began casting a white-and-chartreuse Deceiver, my most reliable striper fly. I was vaguely aware that Keith had heaved something off the stern with his spinning rod and was dragging it behind us. A moment later he grunted. I turned. His rod was bowed. When he cranked the fish in, I saw that it was a large bass. He measured it against some markings on the boat, shrugged, and released it.

"How big?" I said.

"Thirty-two."

"Almost a keeper," I said. "I never caught a keeper. That's my goal. A thirty-six inch bass. I don't want to keep it. I just want to catch one."

He shrugged. "Toy rod," he said.

We fished for an hour, during which time Keith caught five bass. None was quite a keeper, but all were within a few inches on either side of thirty. I changed flies a dozen times and never had a strike. Finally I said, "Let me see what you're using."

A stiff wire leader was threaded through a one-foot length of orange rubber tubing with a sand worm impaled on the hook at the end of the rig. He let it drag beside the boat. It looked like a snake in the water.

"What in hell do you call that?" I said.

"Turkey bone. Wanna try?"

"No, thanks."

"Hang one on your fly rod."

"That's not fly fishing."

"Nope-suh, I guess it ain't."

We chugged up and down the creek for another hour. I continued to get no strikes and Keith landed three more and lost a couple.

"Listen," I said. "Maybe I'll try one of those turkey bones."

"On your toy rod?"

"No. Gimme that other spinning rod."

"You?"

"Sure. I'm not proud."

"Course you ain't."

So I trolled turkey bones from a spinning rod and began to catch stripers, and then I hooked one that felt bigger and stronger than the others. "Keeper," I grunted. "Gotta be." I cranked the handle of the spinning reel one way and the line kept moving the other way, and when I tightened the drag that fish still took line. I couldn't get leverage with the short spinning rod to turn it the way I could have with my ten-weight. Once the fish rolled near the surface and we saw its breadth.

"Oh, my," whispered Keith.

Then it wrapped a piling and was gone.

We continued to troll turkey bones and caught a few more before the tide turned. All nice ones, but no keepers. We chugged silently back toward the landing as darkness gathered over the marsh.

Finally Keith said, "Somethin' wrong?"

I shook my head.

"You're unnaturally quiet."

"I'm thinkin'," I mumbled.

"I get it," he chuckled. "You finally seen the light. Gonna give up that toy rod and go after stripers with real gear, huh?"

"Nope-suh," I said. "Just figurin' how I can tie me a turkey bone fly."

10

Aquatic Agony

"We want to bring attention to the desperate situation fish are in," Tracy Reiman says. "We're planning demonstrations on the docks, at the fishing tournaments, whatever. This is the final frontier for the animal rights movement."

Ms. Reiman is the national organizer of the PETA (People for the Ethical Treatment of Animals) antifishing crusade, and she means business. "Ultimately," she says, "what we want is for people not to fish."

In the fall of 1995 PETA launched what they euphemistically called a "fishing survey," in which their volunteers confronted folks fishing from piers and asked them such rhetorical questions as "What do you think it feels like to suffocate?"; "Do you think fish should be protected in any way?"; and, "What do you think makes your pet different from fish?"

PETA, of course, had no intention of learning anything from the fishermen they "surveyed." They already had the answers. "We hope to find out why people fish," Reiman admitted. "Then we can talk to them in their own language about switching to a harmless pastime. . . . Many people, even those who live with dogs and cats, haven't considered that fish have nervous systems and pain receptors, and suffer when they are caught."[1]

More confrontational animal rights activists are expressing their views on the pain and suffering of fish by throwing rocks at fishermen and spray-painting antifishing messages on their cars.

The definition of "agony" lies at the heart of PETA's antifishing campaign. Fish, they explain, "are vertebrates with a brain, a central nervous system, and pain receptors all over their bodies, including the lips. . . . All vertebrates are able to experience pain to one degree or another. . . . There is no reason to differentiate between warm-blooded and cold-blooded creatures. . . . Angling inflicts injury, causes pain and trauma to the fish, and

---

[1] "National Fishing Survey Launched," PETA press release. November 3, 1995.

even if the fish is to be returned to the water, death can still result."

PETA, in fact, has targeted catch-and-release angling as particularly abhorrent. "Fishes who are released," they say, "suffer such severe physiological and psychological stress from being played, often for long periods, that they may die even though they manage to swim away, or may be so weakened they are easy prey for other predators. Many trout streams are so intensely fished that they are subject to 'catch and release' regulations requiring that all fishes caught must be let go; the aquatic animals in these streams are likely to spend their entire short lives being repeatedly traumatized and injured."

It's easy to shrug off some of these laughable arguments. Take an animal radical to the Yellowstone River around Buffalo Ford in the park on July 15, opening day, when the trout are very stupid, and then again toward the end of August, after six weeks or so of intense catch-and-release fishing pressure. Those Yellowstone cutthroats do not act traumatized; mostly, they just act smart. Studies have shown that Yellowstone trout are caught and released an average of eleven times apiece in the course of a single season. The health of the Yellowstone fishery has improved dramatically since catch-and-release was inaugurated.

There is no evidence that the lives of these trout are "short" or that they've been "traumatized."

I've had a running battle with animal fanatics since I began writing about hunting more than a decade ago. I've been called "sadistic" and worse because I've glorified the pursuit of New England ruffed grouse and woodcock with a pointing dog and a 20-gauge double-barreled shotgun.

I've argued that the hunting (and, by extension, fishing) instinct evolved from human survival demands and continues to thrive in all our genes. I've written that I'm only doing what's natural, and that those who don't hunt or fish simply find other, sometimes less benign, outlets for this powerful drive. I've pointed out that Nature is cruel, that every creature is both predator and prey, and that fear and pain and suffering and death are the natural order of things.

I've responded to my critics by pointing out that true sportsmen like to mind their own business. They do not bother other people—which is more than can be said for animal-rights activists.

But I've always regretted that hunting inevitably produces the death of the grouse and woodcock that I love. In fact, I've written that I wish I could put back those dead birds, like trout.

When it has come to fishing, though, I've felt virtuous and insulated from the sometimes troubling arguments of the PETA people. I can and do put back the fish I manage to catch.

Still, anyone who grew up on the banks of a willow-shaded creek or pond waiting for a bobber to start dancing on the water—surely one of humankind's most inoffensive activities—must give the PETA thesis serious consideration. That goes double for us fly fishermen, who, we like to think, are among civilization's most contemplative and least sadistic folks. Most of us do not enjoy inflicting discomfort on anyone or anything.

If someone tells us we are causing "agony," we should take them seriously.

Like the rest of the animal rights agenda, the concept of "aquatic agony" rests on the anthropomorphic assumption that all organisms feel and think the same way people do. According to this argument, animals of all species are like us; they just happen to look different. Regardless of their position on the food chain, they all experience emotions equivalent to what we know as love, fear, and pain. Ever since the movie *Bambi* jerked tears from a generation of children, the differences between us and other creatures have been blurry.

According to PETA "research," fish "do not express pain and suffering in ways that humans easily recognize (although they indeed gasp and struggle when caught). . . . Fishes' lips and tongues can be compared to human hands . . . fishes use them to catch or gather food, build nests, and even hide their offspring from danger. These uses require a well-developed tactile sensitivity that is severely damaged by needle-sharp barbed hooks. Hooked fishes struggle out of fear and physical pain."[2]

More than two thousand years ago, the Greek poet Bion said: "Though boys throw stones at frogs in sport, the frogs do not die in sport, but in earnest." The same goes for anglers and trout. We use the euphemistic word "play" to describe what we do when we hook a fish. Unlike the PETA folks, I don't pretend to know what goes through the "mind" of a hooked trout. But I doubt if he thinks of it as play.

As dubious as some of PETA's arguments are, we "sport" fishermen should not discount them entirely. "Playing" large fish for a long time on unnecessarily light tackle surely overstresses them, and while it may give the angler a kick, it is not sporting. Reserve your one-weight outfit for little beaver-pond

[2] "Fishing: Aquatic Agony," PETA On-Line.

brookies and bluegills. Squeezing fish, holding them by their gills, ripping hooks from their mouths, dropping them on the ground or the bottom of the boat, keeping them out of water more than a few seconds, "throwing" them back or, for that matter, returning them to the water when they're bleeding, and generally treating them with disrespect demeans us and them and our beloved pastime. Catch-and-release angling has been the salvation of striped bass and trout, but a fish that is unlikely to recover from being caught should be killed swiftly and humanely, taken home, prepared elegantly, and eaten respectfully. If the well-meaning folks at PETA can raise the consciousness of sport fishermen, they have performed a useful service.

At the same time, we cannot lose sight of the fact that deer and ducks cannot talk, that fear and pain are important survival mechanisms that enable wild creatures to elude their natural predators, and that fish, for Heaven's sake, are not people.

III

Translating from the Latin

Now for flies, which is the third bait wherewith trouts are usually taken. You are to know that there are so many sorts of flies as there be of fruits . . . indeed too many either for me to name, or for you to remember: and their breeding is so various and wonderful, that I might easily amaze myself, and tire you in a relation of them.

—Izaak Walton, *The Compleat Angler*

11

A Fateful Encounter

Like many anglers of my generation (let's just say I have vague childhood memories of ration stamps and VJ Day, and I began fly fishing for trout shortly thereafter), trout fishing meant wading upstream and casting dry flies either to rising fish or to fishy riffles and runs. When I felt reckless and rebellious, I turned around and skittered a dry fly down and across the currents on a tight line.

I didn't pay much attention to fussy hatch-matching. I learned to recognize our major Eastern spring hatches—the Quill Gordons, Hendricksons, March Browns, and Light Cahills—but I didn't bother putting Latin names to them, and I used the same fly for all of them. My father invented it. He believed it suggested all of those naturals well enough to fool trout. It had stripped hackle-quill tails, a peacock-quill body, split wood-duck wings, and mixed ginger and grizzly hackle, tied bushy. He called it the "Nearenuf."

Perhaps because the Neareunf was the only fly I used, it was the only fly I caught trout on, and it seemed, therefore, to be the only fly I needed. During a hatch, I tried to match the size of the natural (although a size fourteen almost always did the trick). Otherwise, I concentrated on making accurate casts and drag-free floats.

I knelt at the altar of Presentation and scoffed at the false god of finicky Imitation. I sneered at talk of spinners and nymphs, emergers and cripples. I accepted the possibility that trout fed on them all, but trying to imitate them seemed unnecessary. "Affectation," I called it, a useful word I'd heard Dad apply to certain fly-fishing (and other kinds of) snobs he knew. Turning over rocks, studying bugs, rummaging in flyboxes, and tying and retying knots—all wasted valuable fishing time.

Fly fishing for trout was a simple sport. Tie on a Nearenuf and keep it on the water. When I didn't catch fish, it wasn't my fault. If they weren't rising, I just said, "They aren't looking up." If I found a surface-feeding fish that I couldn't catch, I went looking for another one.

It was one of those delicious March afternoons in New England when, for the first time in months, I could smell the thawing earth, and the sun actually felt warm on my face. I knew that spring would come after all. The urge to go fishing was irresistible.

So I tossed a rod and a box of flies onto the back seat of my car and drove to my local trout stream. It was a quixotic journey, of course, because I knew the hatchery truck had not yet made its deposit, and this stream did not support native trout. I did not expect to rig up my rod or wet a line. But as I walked the banks, I found bare patches of earth where skunk cabbages had pushed their noses through the blanket of wet leaves, and I flushed a couple of early robins. Sap coursed through the willows and maples, turning their tips yellow and red. Melting snow had not yet swollen the stream, and where it ran low and clear, it reminded me of miniature trout streams.

Being there, on this day, was enough. I felt my own sap rising.

Then a miracle: I spotted a rising trout. He hung suspended just under the surface in a place where a riffle flattened into a pool, and every now and then he darted sideways and lifted his head to eat. He was, I could see, a brown trout, and larger than the run-of-the-mill hatchery fish they stocked here every

April. He had somehow managed to survive the summer drought and the winter freeze, and here he was, welcoming spring with me.

I sat on a boulder to watch, too enthralled, at first, to care about trying to catch him. It felt like a gift, an unlikely promise unexpectedly fulfilled, and the encounter felt prophetic. It couldn't have been a random accident. That brown trout had, I believed, summoned me from my house to the banks of my stream on this springlike March afternoon, and it seemed predestined that I was intended to catch him.

So I strung up my rod, and I tied on a Nearenuf with one eye and watched the trout with the other. He was feeding regularly and greedily, hungry after a long winter. *Easy pickins,* I thought. I knew I would catch him and put him back even before I made my first cast.

I slipped downstream, false-cast, and dropped the Nearenuf five feet above him. It bobbed in the riffle and drifted directly onto his nose. When he didn't take it, I cast again. This time he lifted his nose—and ate something barely an inch from my fly. When he refused a third perfect presentation, I smiled. Okay. Good. I understood. I had been called here to meet a challenge. I had been given a lesson, if I only had the wit to learn it.

So I returned to the boulder and did something I had never done before: I actually studied that trout's behavior and tried to understand exactly what he was doing. And after a while I noticed that when he fed, his head and dorsal fin broke the surface, but his mouth did not. He was, I concluded, eating something just under the surface, not off the top of it.

I knew about nymphs, of course. I'd overheard the esoteric discussions of pseudo-sophisticated anglers. I'd read the articles and books by outdoor writers who were, I figured, desperate for something new to say. It was interesting, in an abstract sort of way. But more affectation. It never seemed to have much to do with actually catching trout. For that, I knew, you only had to tie on a Nearenuf.

Except watching this trout, I was forced to conclude that he was feeding selectively on emerging nymphs, and since he was probably the only trout in the entire stream, if I were going to catch anything on this day, it would have to be this one. And I'd have to do it on a nymph.

I didn't own a nymph assortment. But when I rummaged among my dry flies, I found a dull olive-colored nymph buried under some Nearenufs, and I remembered finding it the previous spring on this same little stream, snagged in a streamside bush with a length of tippet dangling from it. I had cut it loose and dropped it into my box and forgotten about it.

That brown trout was the only fish in the stream, and that drab olive nymph was the only one I owned, itself a gift from the stream. There seemed something enormously fateful about that.

So I tied on my only nymph, lobbed it up into the riffle, and watched the place where my tippet entered the water. As it neared the trout, I saw his dorsal fin lift, his head twist to the side, and his mouth wink white. I reflexively raised my rod and felt, for the first time in six months, the pulse of a fish throbbing in my fingers.

I played him quickly, cradled his belly in my hand, and unhooked him. He was a beautifully spotted brown trout, fourteen or fifteen inches long, and I held him there in the frigid water for a moment to admire him. Then I removed my hand to release him, my gift to the stream.

I took down my rod and headed back to my car. I flushed robins along the way, and I smelled the thawing earth and the pungent skunk cabbages, and I felt the springlike sun, warm on the back of my neck.

And I thought about that trout. It was the first one I had ever really observed, the first one I had ever tried to understand, the first one I had ever caught as a result of deductive reasoning. It was, I thought, the first trout I had ever truly deserved to catch.

It was a powerful lesson and a priceless gift, and I absolutely believed—as I still do—that what happened that March afternoon had not happened at random.

12

Terrestrial Incognito

Bubba and I were creeping upstream tight to the south bank of the Bighorn, hunting sippers.

The riseform of a bank-sipping Bighorn trout resembles the disturbance a blueberry makes when dropped from six inches above the water. If you look closely against the glare, you can see the black silhouette of a triangular nose poke leisurely through the surface. You judge the dimensions of the trout by the size of the tip of his snout.

Bubba calls a big trout a "toad," because that's what his protruding nose looks like.

The PMD hatch had come on schedule, around eleven, and had lasted several hours. Now it had petered out, and the river, which had earlier churned with feeding trout, looked dead. Except to Bubba, who knew the Bighorn never slept. He could always find rising fish. He knew that some of them—the big ones that had taken up feeding positions in shallow water for easy gluttonizing when hatching mayflies littered the water— liked to linger there afterward to scavenge.

There's always plenty of edible crud drifting on the braided Bighorn currents—leftover PMD duns, cripples, stillborns, *baetis* spinners, yellow Sallies, caddis flies, ants, midges. The posthatch sippers never seem particularly choosy. The trick— the exquisite challenge—is to spot one before he spots you, to creep up behind him in ankle-deep water, then to drop a dry fly just two feet upstream of his lie, laying the leader tippet right between his eyes. Do that, and a toad-shaped nose pokes up and eats.

Tighten on him and all hell breaks loose.

Those trout—mostly browns, but often enough rainbows— are the big ones. Eighteen inches is run of the mill. Some of the rainbows are two-footers.

We were wet wading, and the chill of the ankle-deep water had numbed my feet and was shooting cold pains toward my hips. My upper half was sweating hard under the relentless afternoon Montana sun. We were casting Green Weenies, Bubba's imitation of the Blue-Winged Olive spinner, a never-fail pattern for bank sippers. By now, we had caught enough toothy brown trout so that my Green Weenie had lost one wing and the fur dubbing was coming loose, which Bubba said perfectly imitated the bedraggled naturals on the water and gave me an unfair advantage. It fully explained, he declared, the fact that, for once, I was outfishing him.

We took turns. Five casts and out. You could stalk and catch three trout on your five casts, or you could throw five tailing loops and spook five fish and catch nothing. Either way, that was your turn. With your partner crouched by your shoulder whispering advice, criticizing your form, and questioning your heritage, you often catch nothing. Limiting your number of casts strictly to five can give an angler what Bubba calls a "cast-ration complex."

Bubba had just released a ho-hum eighteen-inch brown, which he had taken on his fifth try, and he was blowing on his Green Weenie and humming Handel's "Hallelujah Chorus," when he suddenly pointed with his rod tip. "There, Grandfather," he whispered. "Oh, look at the size of that nose."

I squinted down his rod, and fifteen seconds later I saw it. The fish lay barely a foot from the bank in the shade of an overhanging cottonwood about a hundred feet upstream. He had a nose like a bullfrog.

"Tough lie," I murmured.

"You're the hotshot today," said Bubba. "It's your turn."

We waded up into position, crouched over, moving slowly, our eyes focused on the fish. He tilted up to feed every fifteen seconds, as regular as a metronome. "Easy pickins," said Bubba, just to add a little pressure.

My first try, a measuring cast, fell a foot short. It's better to be short than long. Drop your leader butt on top of a big trout in eight inches of water and you blow him up.

I waited, timing him, then lay my tippet between his eyes. I heard Bubba suck in air. I held my breath. Then the nose came up and ate—a millisecond after my fly had passed over him.

"Damn," muttered Bubba.

Of my next three casts, two were perfect. The trout ignored them all.

"The master's turn," said Bubba, shouldering me aside.

All five of his casts were perfect. The trout continued to rise every fifteen seconds, but he did not eat Bubba's Green Weenie.

"Hm," mumbled Bubba.

"Another fly?" I said.

"Makes no sense. But sure. Try it."

I gave the fish five good looks at a black ant. Then Bubba showed him a caddis. I was halfway through my next turn, and the fish was still feeding and ignoring my fly, when Bubba said, "Aha!"

I turned, and he held his open palm to me. In it lay an insect. It was round, with a fluorescent green body and a red head, size eighteen or twenty.

"What is it, some kind of beetle?" I said.

He shrugged. "Never saw anything that looked like this before in my life. But they're on the water. Must be what that toad is munching on."

"I've got black beetles. No green ones."

"Try a black one."

I did. The trout ignored it.

We never did blow him up, but during Bubba's next turn the trout stopped feeding. We continued to stalk bank feeders, but Bubba spent the rest of the afternoon mumbling to himself. "One thing to spook 'em," he grumbled. "But I don't like to be ignored."

There are nearly three hundred thousand species of beetles on earth. When they appear in a stream, they become trout food.

There are also grasshoppers, ants, flies, crickets, cicadas, and a variety of landlubbing larvae that from time to time fly, fall, or are blown onto the water. They must be delicious and nourishing, because trout gobble them.

My introduction to the appeal of terrestrials came on the Henrys Fork. Bob Lamm and I arrived in the midst of one of those typical complex-compound hatches where the water was littered with several species of mayflies in various stages of emergence. There were drakes and PMDs and sulphurs and *baetis* and midges and half a dozen different caddis flies, plus several species I couldn't identify. There were emergers, duns, cripples, stillborns, and spinners ranging from large to minute, and nymphs and pupae, too. Big noses were poking up among the small ones, and we had no idea what they were eating.

We caught them on ants.

"Why?" I asked Bob.

"Who cares," he said.

A few years ago, Andy Gill and I timed our trip to Utah's Green River to coincide with that tailwater's legendary cicada "hatch." We had tied up dozens of crude imitations—black foam bodies, rubber legs, white bucktail wings with a few strands of Flashabou, several turns of grizzly hackle between abdomen and thorax, on a No. 8 long-shank hook. When we showed them to Mike Howard, our guide, he shrugged. "Close enough," he said.

The woods that bordered the river where it passed through Flaming Gorge buzzed with tree-born insects. Cicadas. But when we launched the driftboat just below the dam, we saw none of the big lumbering bugs in the air or on the water, and we saw no rising trout. "Don't worry about it," said Mike when we mentioned it to him. "Just heave one of those ugly things out there."

"Where?"

"Anywhere."

We did. And we proceeded to have the most disgusting, exhilarating trout-catching orgy of our lives. Every trout in the Green—which, in those days, boasted the biggest pounds-per-mile ratio in the country—had its nose at the surface looking for cicadas, or any big ugly fly that vaguely resembled them. Andy and I don't keep score, but at the end of the day Mike estimated that we'd boated well over one hundred trout between us, all but a few eighteen inches and larger.

"Makes no sense," I said to Mike. "All day, I never saw a single real cicada on the water."

"The trees are full of 'em," he said. "The trout know that."
He shrugged, as if that explained it.

"I see," I said, although I didn't.

When I fished some Pennsylvania limestoners several Septembers ago with Barry and Cathy Beck, Barry handed me one of his chartreuse inchworm imitations. "Try this," he said.

"Why?" I asked. "There haven't been inchworms in the bushes since June."

"Just a suggestion," said Barry quietly. "Use something else if you want."

I muttered, "When in Rome," and tied on the inchworm. I shouldn't have been surprised that the trout gobbled it.

I've caught frustrating midging trout from Eastern tailwaters and Western spring creeks—on beetles and hoppers and crickets, and at times of the year when none of those terrestrial insects were even in the bushes, much less on the water. Such experiences raise serious doubts about the selectivity of trout.

Or maybe not. Maybe trout actually select terrestrials over mayflies and caddisflies and midges, and will glom onto the odd beetle or ant whenever they spot one drifting in the film. Maybe early experiences teach trout that terrestrials are more delicious and nourishing than aquatic insects. Maybe this tidbit of information becomes imprinted in their survival-tuned memories, and is activated at the sight of a foam beetle or fur ant tied to a 6X tippet.

Inch-long cicadas must be loaded with protein. Maybe Green River trout remember that. Maybe formic acid is chocolate to a Henrys Fork trout.

It should be enough for the angler to know that he can fool most trout most of the time with a terrestrial, regardless of what they happen to be actually feeding on. It's comforting knowledge, and it simplifies everything. It works. Why ask why?

I, for one, keep asking why, but so far, nobody's explained it to me.

I had to leave for Massachusetts the day after Bubba and I struck out on the big fish that was eating the little beetlelike bugs with the neon-green bodies and red heads. I should have forgotten about it, because we'd caught lots of fish, but I didn't. I've found that the trout I don't catch are the ones I remember most vividly.

A few days after I got home, I received a note from Bubba. "Dear Grandfather," he wrote. "Tied a crude imitation of that green bug and caught the bank sipper under the cottonwood the day after you left. Fair rainbow, 23½ inches. Asked around about the bug. Someone called it a soldier fly. Can't find it in my bug books. Funny thing. I saw one dry its wings and fly off the water. Makes me think it might be some kind of aquatic insect, not a terrestrial. That would explain it, huh?"

As far as I was concerned, the only thing it might explain was that there is no end to the mysteries we encounter on trout streams. Which, of course, is what keeps us going back.

I tied up a batch of those mysterious bugs, copying the sample that Bubba included with his note. But in all the years since we found that frustrating rainbow sipping under the cottonwood, I've never seen a green-bodied beetle-shaped insect with a red head on the Bighorn, or anywhere else.

Bubba thinks it's an aquatic insect and calls it a soldier bug. I call it "terrestrial, unknown."

13

Small Flies Mean Big Trout

It looked like one of those rare times when chasing a rumor was actually going to pay off. "Giant mayflies," Cliff had whispered to me on the phone. "Some kind of drake, I think. It's started. They hatch around dusk and the trout go bananas."

A rare and wonderful sort of friend, Cliff named the stream and even told me how to find his favorite pool. I got there a little after seven on that soft June evening. And it was true. Huge greenish-yellow mayflies were drifting on the water, drying their wings, and then lumbering into the air. They looked as big as sparrows. And the pool was pocked with the rings of rising trout.

I fumbled a size eight drake paradun onto my 3X tippet and waded in. A businesslike boil thirty feet upstream drew my first cast. My fly settled onto the water five feet upstream of the fish. To my eye the imitation was indistinguishable from the scattering of little schooners on the water. I leaned forward, tensed for the inevitable take. My fly drifted directly onto the trout's nose.

It continued past him.

I cast again. This time he swirled so close to my fly that it rocked in the wake of his rise.

I tried him one more time, and when he ignored my fly for the third time I smiled. It had happened again.

Well, cool. A mystery. Next to catching big trout on big dry flies, sleuthing is one of my favorite trout stream preoccupations.

I bent over and studied the water that flowed past my waders. Now and then a big drake floated by. But for every giant greenish-olive mayfly came several dozen pale yellow ones, which I recognized as sulphurs, a regular and prolific June hatch on my trout streams. They were tiny—about size twenty, I estimated—and most of them were struggling to squirm out of their nymphal skins, barely afloat, so that they were drifting flush in the surface film. From thirty feet, they were invisible.

I returned my attention to the trout upstream of me. Two or three drakes passed over him untouched. When he rose, it was a dainty sip.

This trout, I concluded, had focused his attention on the more abundant little sulphurs, and as I studied the rest of the water around me I spotted several other feeding trout. All of them were gobbling at the surface regularly. I did not see a single big drake get eaten.

I've watched trout ignore big insects in favor of tiny ones enough times that it no longer surprises me.

Aquatic insects, in their many and varied species and in all the stages of their life cycles, provide food for trout and hatch-matching problems for anglers. I doubt if trout consider eating a cerebral exercise, but matching a hatch can be deliciously challenging for the angler.

Actually, there are times when it can be downright infuriating, as Elliot Schildkrout and I discovered one hot August day on a big Western trout river.

The morning spinnerfall had come on schedule, shortly after daybreak. But it fizzled out under the blazing Montana sun, and by midmorning it seemed as if every trout in the river had gone back to bed. We rowed slowly downriver, scanning the water for rising fish. Finally we spotted a few noses poking through the shaded slick currents that the river funneled against the foot of a high bluff. We pulled the driftboat against the bank.

"Oh, yeah," whispered Elliot reverently. "Look at that."

Dozens of trout were sipping quietly, tight against the steep bank. When we looked at the water, we saw pale morning dun, Trico and *baetis* mayfly duns and spinners, black, speckled, and blond caddis flies, yellow Sally stone flies, and a smattering of hoppers and beetles drifting on the surface. It was a trout smorgasbord.

"What do you think they're eating?" I said.

"Anything," said Elliot, already climbing out of the boat. "Everything. It's an all-you-can-eat buffet. Let's get 'em."

We fished side by side, changed flies often, called the fish colorful names, and raised none of them, although they continued to feed from the surface—often within millimeters of our imitations.

After a while I accepted defeat. I reeled in, climbed into the anchored boat, and took a ham-and-cheese sandwich and a jug of lemonade from the cooler. I watched Elliot, more persevering than I, continue casting, changing flies, and mumbling, while I ate. Bugs kept crawling on my face, and I brushed them away. One got in my mouth, and when I spit it out, I must have muttered a curse, because Elliot turned and said, "What'd you say?"

"Damn ants," I said. "They're all over the boat, in my face, on my sandwich."

Small Flies Mean Big Trout

"Ants, huh?"

The next thing I knew, his rod was bent and his reel was screeching. He landed the trout and a moment later had another one on. About then I figured it out.

Ants. The tiniest bugs on the water. They'd ruined my picnic, but they were the trout's banquet.

We should have known. Whether they're rising selectively to a hatch of aquatic insects or gobbling opportunistically on whatever comes their way, trout rarely refuse to eat the odd ant that drifts over them. Even when they're not rising at all, you can often take trout on a floating ant pattern.

Once on Connecticut's Farmington River I found them gobbling tiny cinnamon ants while a streamful of anglers (including me, until I finally figured it out) futilely cast imitations of the large Hendricksons that were hatching in profusion. When blue-winged olives or Tricos (both of which come in sizes twenty and smaller) are on the water, trout usually spurn anything else that may drift over their noses, regardless of how big and juicy it may be. Trout eat the myriad species of midges and small caddis flies virtually year round.

Most of the time, if they have a choice, trout eat small bugs and spurn big ones.

I leaned my elbows on the wooden railing of the bridge and watched the old guy cast. Although I could see no insects on the water, he was surrounded by bulging trout. He cast skillfully. His white-winged dry fly drifted high and drag-free directly over the noses of the gluttonizing fish.

After a few minutes, I called down to him, "How're they bitin'?"

He glanced up at me. "They ain't."

"Looks like they're eating midges," I said.

"Yep. Little black ones."

"What're you using?"

"Royal Wulff."

"But—"

"Hell, I know it's the wrong fly," he said. "But at least I can see it."

I love those times when trout feed on big insects. I've tried to time my Western trips to coincide with the salmonfly hatch on the Madison or the green drakes on the Henrys Fork. Midwesterners mark their calendars for their famous *Hexagenia* hatches. I live for the chance to cast grasshopper or cicada imitations to big brown trout against grassy banks when those bugs are on the water.

Dry-fly fishing is a visual game. You can see the insects on the water, you can pinpoint the location of trout by their riseforms, and you can see your fly as it floats over them. When a trout eats your imitation, much of the thrill comes from being able to witness it. There are those who will argue that you can catch more trout on nymphs, and I'm inclined to agree with them. But you can't beat the excitement of having it all happen at the surface where you can see it.

Therein lies the appeal of casting imitations of the giant, highly visible salmonflies and drakes to surface-feeding trout. For the fisherman, however, there are many problems with these "superhatches": First, they typically last only a week or two; second, they are notoriously unpredictable and unreliable; third, most oversized aquatic insects, for some reason, tend to hatch right at dusk or after dark; fourth, they often hatch so sparsely that the trout pay no attention to them; and, fifth, even when everything seems right, trout often choose to feed on something else anyway.

Small insects (which I define as bugs that I can't see on the water at thirty feet—for these middle-aged eyes, that's usually anything size eighteen or smaller), on the other hand, are trout staples. They hatch at predictable times every day in enormous numbers, in many cases over a period of two months or more. Because the tiny insects are so abundant, trout can fill their stomachs on a single recognizable species while barely moving, and they can do it day after day for many weeks. The dependability of the little flies focuses the notorious selectivity of trout. They develop what some fishermen call a "searching image" or a "predator preference" for these small insects that are so familiar to them.

This is both good news and bad news. The bad news, of course, is that tiny flies are hard to see on the water, thus diminishing the visual pleasures of dry-fly fishing. Small flies also mean wispy tippets, which require fussier knot-tying and more delicate fish-fighting.

The good news, however, outweighs the bad. Because the hatches of tiny insects come predictably and dependably, you can plan trips with confidence, knowing that under normal conditions you will find rising trout, and also knowing what flies to bring with you. In the East, sulphurs hatch virtually every afternoon in May and June, and their spinners fall toward dusk. Pale morning duns begin to hatch at eleven A.M. on most Western rivers in the summer, and they do it every day for six weeks to two months. Trico spinners fall in midmorning during August and September on Eastern and Western rivers, and the various mayflies that are imitated with Blue-Winged Olives hatch from early spring to late autumn.

Midges emerge virtually year-round, as do many of the tiny species of caddis flies. Ants can be found drifting on trout streams from April through September.

Trout need to eat a lot of these little bugs to fill their stomachs, so they tend to hover near the surface and gluttonize aggressively. They get into feeding rhythms that make them easy pickins for an accurately drifted imitation.

Small-fly hatches seem to be scheduled for the fisherman's convenience. Whereas many large flies hatch toward dusk or after dark, small flies typically appear during daylight hours. Even if the drift of your fly is difficult to follow, at least it's easy to spot rises and tie knots.

Many fishermen shy away from using a tiny dry fly, reasoning that since they can't see it, they can't tell when a trout has taken it. It can be frustrating to cast to a feeding fish, see him rise, and belatedly realize that he took your fly.

Nobody actually masters small-fly fishing. It's always challenging, frequently frustrating, and sometimes downright aggravating. But I've picked up a few tricks along the way that have reduced my frustration and improved my odds when trout are eating midges, ants, or minuscule mayflies or caddis flies:

➤ I wear polarized glasses with amber lenses. They don't necessarily help me see my fly on the water, but with them I can follow my leader tippet through the water's glare to my fly's approximate location, and the high contrast of amber sometimes enables me to observe the behavior of fish under the water's surface.

➤ I slightly offset all hooks size twenty and smaller, which seems to increase my percentage of hookups.

➤ I use long (three- or four-foot) leader tippets, and I've lost my reluctance to taper down to 7X or even 8X. Long, slender tippets reduce the chance of drag so present with tiny flies, and the longer they are, the more they will stretch to neutralize my typical heavy-handedness when I've hooked a fish.

➤ I take special pains to tie good knots. Nothing fancy. Threading a 7X tippet through the eye of a size twenty-four hook is hard enough, and the fewer times I have to do it the better I like it. A properly tied improved clinch knot is easy and quick and strong. For tying tippet to leader, the surgeon's knot is much easier than a barrel knot, and, according to Lefty Kreh, stronger. I've found that unless I lubricate my knots before pulling them tight, flimsy tippets tend to kink or weaken at the knot.

➤ I search the flat water for feeding trout. I can locate a floating fly better on smooth, slow-moving currents. I look near the banks and inside current seams. Fortuitously, during heavy hatches, large trout tend to move into quiet water where they don't have to fight heavy currents and where they, like me, can spot floating insects better.

➤ I make short casts. I've found that if I wear drab clothing, wade cautiously, and stalk feeding trout from downstream, I can usually creep to within twenty or thirty feet of them. From that distance even tiny flies are often visible.

➤ I don't flock shoot. During heavy hatches of small flies, trout tend to gather in pods in prime feeding stations. Many times I've had a dozen or more trout gorging right in front of me. I try to resist the temptation to cast blindly among them. Instead, I target a single trout. I cast as precisely as I can. With hundreds of natural insects drifting to them, trout do not need to move far to find food, and they won't move for my fly, either.

➤ Before I cast, I pause to gauge my target trout's feeding rhythm. Fish that are eating heavily tend to rise at regular and predictable intervals, so I try to resist the impulse to begin flailing away until I have determined the trout's pattern. I actually count the seconds between rises, and I time my cast so that my fly will drift onto his nose precisely when it's his time to rise. Then when he does come up, I always raise my rod to set the hook, whether or not I can actually see if it's my fly he's eaten. I follow Bill Rohrbacher's wisdom: "No guts, no glory." When in doubt, I assume it's my fly that's been taken.

→ When I can, I fish down- and across-stream. I make a quartering downstream cast and then raise my rod to drag my fly up and across the currents until it's positioned directly upstream of my trout. Then I lower my rod, shake a little slack into my line, and allow my fly to float down to him. Dragging the fly this way enables me to locate it, making it easier to follow as it drifts to the fish. I do believe that trout eat more confidently when the fly precedes the leader. I've tried to train myself to pause an extra beat before lifting my rod when a trout sips my fly from downstream to avoid pulling it out of his open mouth. This is a challenge to my self-control that I have yet to master.

→ Sometimes (though, I admit, reluctantly) I use visual aids. A strike indicator at the tippet knot about three feet from the fly helps me to locate my fly. Even if I can't actually see the fly, the indicator tells me approximately where it is, and I've trained myself to set the hook if a fish rises in that vicinity. I use the smallest indicator that I can see so that it won't interfere with my casting or presentations. Most of the commercial stick-on indicators are too big. I cut one in half to get the right size.

➤ Small flies call for light tackle, long leaders, and wispy tippets. A three- or four-weight outfit is ideal. I like rods with "soft" action and reels with light silky drags for this work, and double-tapered lines are best for delicate presentations. A twelve-foot leader plus three or four feet of tippet is about right. For flies in sizes sixteen to twenty, I use 6X tippets; for sizes twenty-two and smaller, I go down to 7X.

➤ Hooking and landing large fish on small flies and light tippets demands care. I try to avoid the sudden jerks and tugs that cause break-offs. I've found that I need only to tighten my line to drive a tiny hook firmly into a trout's jaw. Hard experience has taught me that if I rear back on my rod when a trout takes my fly, I'll bust him off. I play all but the smallest trout off the reel. When he wants to run, I let him go. But I still play even large trout aggressively. Today's tippet material is incredibly strong—even 6X stands up to the powerful pull of a strong trout provided I apply even pressure.

When I talked to Cliff the following morning, I said, "You were right. Those big drakes were hatching right where you said they'd be. I landed two nice browns. It was great."

"I'm gonna get out there tonight," he said. "I love those big flies."

I decided not to tell him that the pair of sixteen-inchers I caught took size twenty sulphur emergers. I figured he'd enjoy figuring that out for himself.

14

Mismatching the Hatch

They were sipping tiny mayflies off the glassy surface of the stream. Selective, educated trout. Big ones. The kind of dry-fly challenge I welcome.

But as this particular challenge evolved through the stages of bewilderment to frustration to utter exasperation, I found myself yearning for a hand grenade. I wanted to teach those snotty trout a lesson.

I found no grenade in my fly box. The closest thing I had was a big olive Woolly Bugger. So I tied it on, lobbed it into the middle of that pod of trout, and muttered, "Take that!"

They did. Seven of them took it. I landed five.

It was a revelation.

Usually a fly that's a close representation of the insect they're feeding on will, if you can make it drift naturally on the water, catch trout. But because trout are as whimsical and unpredictable as people, there are times when the best imitation is simply not close enough to fool them. You can play the hatch-matching game with them if you want. But it's a losing proposition.

Sometimes a beetle or ant or hopper will get their attention. I know a few stubborn old-timers who use nothing but a Royal Wulff regardless of what insect trout have selected to feed on, and sometimes these guys catch trout when my best efforts at hatch-matching fail.

I've asked them how they account for their success. They either launch into a lecture on the importance of presentation as compared to imitation, or they shrug and mumble something about trout not being as smart as they're cracked up to be.

Whatever. Royal Wulffs usually don't work for me.

In the absence of hand grenades, when trout are getting the better of me I tie on a streamer.

I once accepted the conventional wisdom that there were only a few conditions when streamers would take trout—early in the season before the mayflies began to hatch, in rising discolored water, on the dark of a summer's moon, or in the autumn when the browns were spawning and aggressive. I believed that streamers would work only in certain rivers, or only in particular kinds of water.

Trout, however, are the same fish, whether they live in tiny meadow streams, broad tailwaters, or tumbling freestoners. They all must eat to survive, and large ones, no matter how cautious and brainy, are always on the lookout for a bellyful in a single bite. Experience has taught me that trout will fall for streamers in any water under almost any conditions.

I now use streamers in big brawling rivers and placid little spring creeks. I fish streamers at all times of day and night, during all seasons of the year, in all kinds of weather, and under all water conditions. I even tie on a streamer when selective surface-feeders refuse my dry-fly efforts. And I've caught trout in all these situations—sometimes very large trout. I've concluded that, if I were forced to fish with only one kind of fly, a streamer would give me the best chance to catch a big trout, regardless of the conditions.

Small trout feed almost exclusively on insects. By the time they grow to a foot in length, however, they eat minnows and other larger prey at least part of the time. If they didn't, they'd find themselves expending more calories catching food than they could consume by digesting it, and they would not survive.

Because baitfish do not "hatch" the way insects do, trout tend to eat them when and where they appear. They do not scrutinize this kind of prey the way they do drifting insects. If they did, they'd lose their chance. They respond to the appearance of a nourishing mouthful quickly, instinctively, and aggressively. If it looks and acts edible, they'll generally eat it.

The key to successful streamer fishing is to activate the trout's predatory instinct. Trout will not strike any old thing that swims nearby. The fly must look alive, vulnerable, and nutritious. Catching trout on streamers depends on the design of the fly and, even more important, on the way it's presented. Proper presentation requires reading the water to determine where the trout lie, fishing the streamer at the right depth, and retrieving it with a seductive action.

Classically, a streamer is cast across the current, swung on a tight line through an across-and-down arc, then stripped in. Trout may hit any time, but they seem to favor the moment when the fly pauses downstream at the end of the swing. The across-and-down method works well in riffles, runs, and pocket water if it's no deeper than three or four feet, because worked this way, the streamer will ride near the surface. I begin at the top of the run and work downstream, taking one step after each cast. I can cover virtually all the water this way.

After the streamer completes its swing, I continue to fish out these across-and-down casts. When my fly lies directly below me, I twitch it forward and then let it fall back a little and rest there for a moment, as if it were a minnow struggling against the current. By simultaneously moving my rod tip from side to side, I can make my streamer cover a wide swath of water. When the fly drifts into a particularly likely downstream spot— beside or in front of a boulder, over a depression on the river bottom, or along a current seam—I pause in the retrieve. I twitch the streamer forward, let it fall back, and maneuver it from side to side, all the while imagining the large trout that's eyeing it, growing increasingly aggressive and hungry.

When trout are lying close to the banks or against bankside obstructions, I try to keep the streamer broadside to the fish for as long as possible. Casting to the bank and pulling the fly back toward the middle of the river gives the trout very little opportunity to see it and decide to eat it. I like to cast slightly upstream and immediately throw a downstream mend into my line, making the fly swim downstream parallel to the bank.

Large predatory trout lurk in deep, turbulent currents, waiting to engulf wayward baitfish. The angler's challenge is to sink his imitation deep enough while making it move in the water with the right action. A full-sinking line with a stubby leader will take the fly deep. A forty- or fifty-foot length of sinking line slicing through several different currents, however, gives the fisherman poor control of both line and fly. A floating line with a weighted fly allows the angler to mend line and hold much of it off the water, while still getting the fly down to the fish. Streamers with lead eyes or lead-wrapped bodies do not cast gracefully, but they plummet to the bottom where the trout live. An unweighted streamer can be made to sink by pinching a large split shot onto the leader right at its nose.

In deep fast water I like to cast a weighted fly on an up-and-across angle and allow it to sink as it sweeps abreast of me before beginning a slow retrieve. Pulsating marabou or rabbit-strip streamers can be cast almost directly upstream and fished on a dead drift, like a nymph. I try to maintain just enough tension in the line to keep contact with the fly. Water currents impart sufficient action to these flies to make them wiggle, tumble, and lurch like injured or disoriented baitfish.

When weighted flies are retrieved with short, sharp jerks, they undulate up and down in a manner that trout often cannot resist. Jigging a weighted streamer even works in slow-moving, clear water. I like to drop a small Woolly Bugger into a pool, let it lie on the bottom for a moment, then lift it a couple of inches and let it drop back. Trout dart out from cover to grab it on the fallback, and sometimes even as it rests motionless on the bottom.

When I've spotted a trout, or when I can read the water and make a good guess where the fish might be lying, I avoid casting my streamer so that it moves directly toward him. Trout expect their prey to flee, not attack them. I try to present my fly so that my target trout can see it, and then I retrieve it so that it angles away from him.

Twitching and pumping with the rod creates moments of slack line that can produce failed hookups. When I retrieve a streamer, I always keep my rod tip low and use my stripping hand, rather than the rod itself, to impart action to the fly. I believe I connect with a higher percentage of strikes this way. I set the hook by pulling back on the line rather than lifting the rod. This way, when I fail to hook the fish, the fly remains in his vicinity where he may strike it again.

The streamer fisherman must be patient and flexible. When I'm convinced that I've located the lair of a large trout, I'm willing to change flies many times. I try different sizes, colors, and designs. I present them at different depths and from different angles. I vary the retrieve—long slow strips, short twitches, up-and-down jigs, dead drift.

I'm convinced that much of the time the streamer pattern makes no difference whatsoever. But since I never know when it's one of those times, I follow several general principles when deciding what to tie on:

→ When the water is high or discolored, I choose large, bulky streamers in dark colors, especially combinations of black and purple. Muddler-type streamers with spun wool or deerhair heads "push" water, sending out vibrations that attract fish when visibility is poor.

→ In low, clear water, on the other hand, I've found that slim, sparsely dressed streamers in shades of white, tan, and pale green work best. Baitfish imitations scarcely an inch long frequently fool even the most skittish trout.

→ Under normal water conditions, I choose small, light-colored flies under bright sunshine, and larger, darker streamers if it's overcast or at night.

➤ Whenever a particular species of baitfish predomi-
nates, I try to match them in size, color, shape, and behavior. In
many Western rivers, for example, sculpins are the trout's
favorite forage. Sculpins range in color from olive to black and
are distinguished by their broad heads and poor swimming abil-
ity. Muddlers, retrieved slowly and allowed to tumble in the
currents, imitate them well.

➤ In various colors and sizes, the good old Woolly
Bugger will meet virtually all streamer needs. Nothing beats the
tantalizing movement of marabou in the water, and because the
Bugger shows the fish no flat sides, it gives them an enticing
profile from all angles. Streamers tied from bunny strips and
Jack Gartside's "soft-hackled streamers" are also deadly.

➤ The traditional "streamer" has feather wings,
which breathe and undulate seductively. In the water, however,
the wings tend to separate from the body in an unnatural manner, and they often get fouled in the bend of the hook during
casting. I reserve my classical featherwing streamers for trolling.

➤ Bucktails do not pulsate as dramatically as marabou
and feathers do. But there are times when the streamlined profile and more subtle action of a sparsely tied bucktail is exactly
what trout are looking for.

➤ Although a little glitter usually enhances a streamer's appeal, too much flash—especially in clear water under bright sunlight—sends trout scurrying for cover. I carry streamers with varying amounts of Flashabou or Krystal flash in the wings. Sometimes I cut it all off.

➤ Predatory fish such as trout key on the eyes and the flared gills of their quarry. I believe that painted or stick-on eyes and a touch of red behind the head enhance the attractiveness of all streamers.

➤ Sometimes I double my odds by using two streamers at a time. I tie a small light-colored fly to my leader, clinch-knot a two-foot length of tippet directly to the bend of the hook, and then tie a larger dark-colored streamer to the other end of the tippet. This rig does not seem to tangle when casting as often as most dropper combinations seem to.

➤ On unfamiliar water, I have no pride whatsoever. I seek out the locals and follow their suggestions, even when they don't make sense to me. One of the most important things I've learned about fishing is that there's plenty I don't know and a lot I can't seem to figure out. I've saved a lot of trial-and-error time by tying on the hot local fly.

Mismatching the Hatch

I'm always confident that if I find the right combination of pattern and strategy, I can snag a hook-jawed predator on a streamer, regardless of the situation—even if he's daintily sipping tiny nymphs or floating insects. I've done it more than a few times.

When I've failed, it's because I haven't solved the puzzle—although that doesn't stop me from sometimes wishing I carried an assortment of hand grenades in my flybox.

15

Tap's Bug

As much as I love being teased and aggravated by picky trout—and outwitting them with tiny flies on flimsy gear—I've never lost my lust for buggin' for bass.

If we anthropomorphize them, trout are brainy and fickle. Bass, on the other hand, are impetuous and hostile.

Unless you've seen a hole appear on the flat surface of a pond where your deerhair bug rested a moment earlier, you probably don't know what I'm talking about.

You can arguably catch more—and bigger—bass under the surface. The bass-boat brigades, with their assortments of spinnerbaits, pig-and-jigs, and rubber worms, have proven this. A dedicated fly rodder can probably do as well as the hardware-throwers with Woolly Buggers and other big subsurface attractors.

But, frankly, I have little enthusiasm for that. It's the sight of that boiling strike, that sudden implosion in the water, that keeps me going after bass. I like paddling the shoreline of a bass pond before sunup, or after sunset, when the water lies as flat and dark as carbon paper. I like casting something light on medium-weight tackle, something that floats so I can see what's going on. I like to twitch it once or twice, give it a burble, then let it sit there while the rings spread and dissipate, imagining the bass that has drifted under it and is eyeing it, trying to decide . . .

If conditions aren't right for casting deerhair bugs on trout gear, I simply don't bother going bass fishing.

In the beginning, Ernest H. Peckinpaugh created the Night Bug. The beginning, for our purposes, came sometime shortly after the turn of the century, and the Night Bug was a cork-bodied bucktail streamer tied on a double hook. Peckinpaugh's bugs took Tennessee bream toward evening when they began to spat for insects on the surface of his local ponds. When he discovered that largemouth bass were attracted to Night Bugs, he began to tie them on larger hooks. Thus was born surface-fishing for bass with the fly rod.

When the Great War cut off Peckinpaugh's supply of double hooks, he adapted his creation to the single hook. Sometime in the 1920s, Will H. Dilg of Chicago happened upon the Night Bug. Dilg experimented with a variety of designs, and his magazine articles popularized the sport of bass-bugging with cork-bodied poppers.

Soon thereafter the magical properties of deerhair were discovered. Spun tightly onto a hook and trimmed to shape, deerhair floated—well, like a cork. Fly tiers, probably feeling that carving and gluing cork qualified more as cabinetmaking than fly tying, adapted deer hair to bass-bug design. Early deerhair bugs were aerodynamic monstrosities that required heavy tackle and linebacker shoulders to cast. But they glugged and gurgled on the surface, and bass crashed them.

Design refinements came quickly. The Calmac Moth moved quietly on the water's surface, suggesting a large insect. Joe Messinger designed his elegant and still-popular Hair Frog, and Roy Yates invented the muddlerlike Deacon.

They all, of course, caught bass. But none quite satisfied my father. Neither the cork-body bugs nor the bulky deerhair designs, which typically came with outrigger wings and big featherduster tails, were pleasant to cast. The moth variations didn't make the surface disturbance that Dad thought attracted predatory bass. Tying Messinger frogs was fussy and time-consuming—and when he made a good one, he considered it too beautiful to fish with.

"Until Roy Yates sent me one of his Deacons," he says, "I mostly used a bait-casting rod and Jitterbugs or Magic Minnows to catch bass on the surface. The Deacon converted me to fly-rod bass bugging, mainly because I found I could cast it comfortably on a five- or six-weight trout rod. I caught a lot of bass on the Deacon. But I kept wondering how I could improve it."

My father made a career out of inventing and refining and simplifying and generally improving things. For thirty-five years he shared his thoughts and creations in his "Tap's Tips" column for *Field & Stream,* and I can report from extensive personal experience that he was—and still is—a compulsive tinkerer. In fact, in 1946 he wrote a book called *Tackle Tinkering* (the title *Tinkle Tackering* by H. G. Tipply . . . no, that's not it . . . inspired one of Ed Zern's most hilarious columns).

"The best feature of the Deacon," says Dad, "was its streamlined shape. It cast as comfortably as a streamer fly. But I felt it didn't kick up enough of a fuss on the surface due to its little round head. And there wasn't enough clipped deerhair on it to keep it afloat very long. So I began experimenting."

His early efforts featured a full-length clipped deerhair body, with a flat bottom and a wide, rounded front end tapered to a point at the rear. He left whiskers at the head and made a tail of flared hackle feathers. "I soon cut off those whiskers," he says. "Too air-resistant for pleasant casting, and they tended to twist the leader and make the thing land upside down. To get the kind of burble I wanted, I left the face flat rather than rounding it off. I fiddled with the tail. The hackle feathers gave it a nice leggy action, but they made the thing whistle and spin when I cast it. I tried bucktail, but getting a nice smooth transition from the tail into the deerhair body was difficult. Finally I found some long deer bodyhair that worked beautifully for the tail. I tie it in right at the butts, and they flare to form the beginning of the body. If there's any secret to tying one of these things, it's using the right deerhair for the tail. It's got to be hollow at the butt ends, and it should be long and fine at the tips so the tail end of it doesn't flare too much." He shrugs. "All the rest is spinning and packing and hedge-trimming the deerhair. It's kind of fun. I can make one in about twenty minutes."

I've been watching my father tie his bugs since I was old enough to climb onto his lap and make half hitches, and although he has always kept me well supplied with Tap's Bugs (as he did dozens of fly-casting bass fishermen across the country), I've tied plenty of them myself. Next to his beautifully symmetrical creations, mine tend to look misshapen and amateurish. But the bass do not seem to discriminate.

Besides finding the right hair for the tail, the only "trick" to making one of Tap's Bugs is to get that flared deerhair packed densely onto the bare hook shank. Dad spins on a drinking-straw-sized bundle, ties it off with a half hitch, and then, pinching the base of the tail tightly between his left thumb and forefinger, he uses his right thumb and forefinger to twist and push the flared hair back. "Don't be gentle with it," he said. "Use strong thread. You want that deerhair compressed as tight as you can get it. I feel that I can cram it tighter with my fingers than with a packing tool. The denser it is, the neater it will be when you trim it and the longer your bug will float."

The flat face, Dad says, makes all the difference in his bug's behavior. "It doesn't pop," he says. "I always felt a loud pop such as you get from some hard-bodied bugs is just as likely to spook a bass as attract him. But a flat-faced deerhair bug plows through the water and burbles when you twitch and retrieve it, and it seems to drive bass nuts. I believe, though I couldn't prove it, that bass are less likely to spit out a soft lifelike deer-hair bug than a hard-bodied cork or balsa popper."

Back in the 1970s Dad sent some of his bugs to his outdoor-writing colleague Charles Waterman. The author of *Fly Rodding for Bass* wrote back: "Last week we used your bugs, together with poppers, on Lake Okeechobee, and yours were winners by a considerable margin." Others who've tried them report similar results.

Dad ties his bugs on 2/0 hooks for largemouths and size 1 hooks for smallmouths. Color? "I like yellow or white simply because I can see it better," he says, "and when I make 'em in other colors I often put some white or yellow at the face for the same reason. But natural gray works fine. Charley Waterman says that in his experience all-white seems to work best for smallmouths." He shrugs. "Personally, I doubt that color makes a bit of difference to the fish."

But besides being a tinkerer, Dad also has a streak of the artist in him, so a box of Tap-tied bugs will contain many combinations of red, green, yellow, orange, red, white, and black. By alternating colors as he spins on the dyed hair, he produces striped effects. He can mingle yellow and green in ways that give his bugs a froglike appearance, and yellow and black looks a lot like a bumblebee. "But these things don't imitate anything," he insists. "I fool around with color combinations just for the fun of it. Make 'em glug and gurgle so they act like something alive and vulnerable. It's the burble that triggers strikes, not the color."

Dad keeps his rod tip pointing at the bug and retrieves it by tugging at the line rather than lifting his rod. After a few casts, the deerhair absorbs some water and rides lower. This actually enhances the burble. When the bug becomes waterlogged, as it eventually does, he simply squeezes the water out of it and resumes casting.

"I look for flat water and shade," he says. "I think bass are reluctant to strike surface lures or flies in the bright sun, and too much ripple neutralizes the fish-attracting commotion of the bug. Early morning and evening, sheltered shores, soft cloudy days with maybe a little mist falling—those are bass-bugging conditions."

A six-weight fly rod loaded with a weight-forward (bass-bug taper) floating line and an eight-foot leader tapered to about 1X makes the ideal outfit for casting Tap's bugs.

Dad always crimps down the barbs on his bugs. "I never keep bass," he says, "and they sometimes inhale the bug and get it deep—especially the smallmouths, for some reason. When they get it in their throats, I just cut the leader and let them keep the bug."

I grew up fishing with my father for both largemouths and smallmouths all over New England. Tap's Bug is about all I've ever used when surface fishing for bass, and lately I've found that it works equally well for schoolie stripers. Miniature bugs are ideal for bluegills, especially with the addition of a few rubberlegs. Pickerel, northern pike, and bluefish crash big long-tailed versions (although it doesn't take many of those toothy critters to shred a bug). Once in Labrador a five-pound brook trout pounced on the pike-sized bug I was glugging through some lily pads.

I enjoy casting Dad's aerodynamic bug almost as much as catching bass on it. A good bass shore offers an infinite variety of targets. Here I drop the bug at the base of a stump or into a pocket among the lily pads. Next I throw a hard tight sidearm loop and skip it under overhanging brush into a dark hole against the bank. I drive it under a dock or bounce it off a boulder. I plop it among the dead limbs of a fallen tree. I crawl it back. It burbles. It rests. It twitches and glugs across the water's still surface.

And no matter how tense and expectant I am, the sudden boil that engulfs my bug never fails to startle me.

IV

Are You Here to Have Fun— Or to Fish?

As no man is born an artist, so no man is born an angler.

—Izaak Walton, *The Compleat Angler*

16

The Magic Hour

Several Junes ago Rip Cunningham, master angler, cast his Deceiver in my direction. "The stripers," he told me on the phone, "are back. Matter of fact, they're all over the place."

"They're really back, huh?"

"Yeah." He gave his fly a couple of seductive twitches. "They're sloshing on the surface and cruising the flats on the first couple hours of the incoming tide. We've been catching lots of them on fly rods."

"Lots? Really?"

"Oh, yeah." Another twitch. "My brother-in-law and I got about forty the other morning."

"Forty! Oh, boy. And on a fly rod."

"Big ones, too," he said. "Keepers, some of 'em. Of course, we released them anyway. They might still be around. Anyway, there are plenty of others." He began to reel in. "But you're a trout guy. Probably not interested . . ."

I was afraid that Deceiver would get away. "No. Wait. I'm interested."

"Yep," he said dreamily. "At least forty. Maybe more. We stopped counting."

I bit. "Just tell me where and when."

"Duxbury launch. Saturday. Four o'clock."

"That's four—"

"A.M.," he said. "Four in the morning, pal. We'll hit the tide perfectly."

I thrashed around a little, but he had me hooked solidly. "Okay," I gulped. "I'll be there."

In my youth I was a confirmed night person. I did my most creative and efficient work in those purple hours after midnight. As I grew older it changed. For a while there I was a morning person. Nothing ridiculous. Eight to one saw me at my best, such as it was.

Lately—well, until I started fishing for striped bass with Rip, I would've said I maybe hit my peak around ten in the morning and faded rapidly after ten-thirty.

The Magic Hour

Now I don't know what you'd call me. But I love to be outdoors during that magic time that's called "first light," about an hour before sunrise.

Rip Cunningham made me a convert. Oh, I still need a little persuading, and without vats of hot black coffee it doesn't work. You can't talk me into getting up to meet a six o'clock tee time, or to go jogging, or to catch an early commuter train, or to make breakfast for the kids. At least not voluntarily.

But tell me that black ducks flock to decoys at sunrise on a salt marsh in December, or that trout swarm in the shallows at daybreak to sip spinners off the surface of a spring creek in June, or that big bass prowl the misty surfaces of a weedy bass pond in August, when the stars are just beginning to fade—and I'll be there.

And I'll feel virtuous as hell about it. I've got the jump on all of you, I want to shout at the dark houses I pass along the way. You're laggards, and I'm not. By the time you roll out of bed, I will have beat you to a big chunk of the day. Go ahead. Sleep. I'm living. I've got too much to do. I'll catch up on my rest when the Big Sleep comes.

"The morning," said Thoreau, "which is the most memorable season of the day, is the awakening hour. Then there is least somnolence in us; and for an hour, at least, some part of us awakes which slumbers all the rest of the day and night."

Somehow the world feels a lot different when I'm leaving for an outdoor rendezvous at three on a summer's morning than it does when I'm coming home at that hour.

Sometimes I don't even bring a rod. I just like to beat the sunrise to the banks of the same pond that will, I know, erupt in a few hours with boom boxes and water skiers and squalling children and screaming parents. Before dawn, a soft mist blankets the water. A pair of mallards—a duck and her drake—lead a ragged string of ducklings along the shore. Their wakes trail out thirty yards behind them. A few tired bullfrogs grumble among the lily pads, and bats and swallows dart after the midges and mosquitoes that cloud over the water, looking for a bedtime snack. The black head of a muskrat vees across a cove. A heron stands statuelike, knee-deep among the rushes.

Overhead the stars begin to wink out one by one. I sit quietly and watch the new day's color bleed into the pewter sky—pale yellow first, merging into orange, then pink, painting the clouds and reflecting on the water's flat surface.

The birds never sing as enthusiastically as they do in the summer woods just before dawn, when the mingled melodies of two dozen species make a symphony. I can taste the sweetness of the moist morning air and feel it caress the fine hairs on my arms.

When I sit on the bank of a pond or a stream at daybreak, I can catch a whole day's limit of life even when I leave my rod home. I have Rip Cunningham to thank for that.

I left at two-thirty and drove in the dark to Duxbury. All those other cars on the highway were headed home, I figured. They were at the end of something; I was at the beginning.

We loaded the boat by flashlight and maneuvered among the black silhouettes of moored sailboats and yachts. A bell buoy clanged hollowly in the misty darkness. Gulls screeched. We cleared the harbor as the night began to fade, and we beached Rip's boat on a low-tide sand island just as the first line of pink appeared in the east.

Rip pointed. "There," he whispered. "Let's go!"

Wakes. Swirls. Shadows. Here and there, a tail waving in the air. Stripers, big ones, chasing bait, cruising the flats, and, yes, eating our flies.

We caught a lot of fish in the twilight. Then the sun cracked the eastern horizon. It happened suddenly and all at once. Day—literally—broke, and the night was abruptly gone. And I was there to see it. It was magic.

17

Fishing in the Dark

It didn't start until after the sun sank behind the Vermont hills and dusk faded from gray to purple to black. First came the bats and swallows, materializing out of the darkness, swooping and darting over the water, sometimes skimming their wingtips on its surface. The trout didn't begin to rise until the stars popped out in a moonless sky. At first I couldn't distinguish their riseforms from the natural eddies and braids of current. But gradually, as my eyes adjusted, I began to detect the silent splashes and swirls of feeding trout. They captured shards of light from the sky, spread them over the inky slickness of the water's surface, and expanded them until they dissipated.

Against the night sky I could see smoky clouds of insects floating over the river. Caddis, maybe. Or a spinner fall. Back then, about thirty years ago, I didn't know much about either. And it didn't matter. The bushy gray dry fly on the end of my leader would have to do, because I couldn't tie on another. I didn't have a flashlight with me.

I had cast that fly over the most likely-looking runs of this stretch of the upper Connecticut River all afternoon. The August sun beat down on the water, and I had seen no fish. But the river looked as good as its reputation, and I had come far to test it. I was reluctant to quit. So I kept casting while the sun descended and the air cooled. And now it was night and everything was different.

I cast out into the current. I squinted hard, looking for those mottled wings that had been so visible in the afternoon sunlight. Impossible. My fly floated, I assumed, through the line of feeding trout in front of me. Maybe not. Maybe it was nowhere near them. Or maybe one of those fish had taken it under and spit out. As hard as I looked, I simply couldn't see what was going on.

But I kept casting out into the darkness, following what I imagined to be the drift of my fly, picking up, casting again, and after a while I gave up trying to see. I allowed the night to wash over me. Gradually I realized that I could smell the river, a clean, moist, almost odorless smell, but a smell, nevertheless. And I sensed the air on my face and arms, soft and liquid and black.

And, for the first time in my life, I heard the tiny sucking noises of surface-feeding trout, and I heard their swirls and splashes when their noses and tails broke through the skin of the river.

I continued to cast, by sound now, and once, for some reason that my brain did not explain to my mind, my arm twitched and my rod jerked and a throbbing vibration traveled up the fly line to my hand. I didn't understand what had happened. I had seen nothing. But somehow I had raised and hooked a trout.

I played him in the darkness. I might as well have closed my eyes. But when he came ghosting to my feet I saw the silvery glint of him, and I knew that it was a rainbow fourteen or fifteen inches long.

I released him, blew on my fly, and cast again. And soon another trout was jerking and tugging on my line. And then I began to understand what was happening. I had switched off the part of my mind that was governed by vision. I had allowed my other senses to take control. By feel, I was able to cast the proper distance so that my fly would float over those rising trout. My casting, I sensed, was perfect, as it rarely was in daylight. The feel of the rod moving though that tangible night air created a picture I could see only in my mind's eye—my fly line lifting off the river, rolling back over my shoulder, straightening, pausing, uncurling in a graceful loop over the river, then settling softly like a slender snake onto its surface. By feel I sensed when to mend my line. Senses other than sight enabled me to follow the drift of my fly.

It might have been my ears that told me when a trout had taken it. Somehow I knew, with an accuracy that seemed extrasensory, exactly which barely audible slurp was the one that had come to my fly. Or maybe it was a new sensitivity in my fingers that transmitted a sudden, subtle twitch of life in the line I held that caused my wrist to jerk instinctively. I don't know. But for an hour or more I hooked a trout on every third or fourth cast. As long as I was able to blank my mind, to forget everything I had learned about reacting to what I could see, to turn the mechanics of fishing over to my senses of touch and sound, I caught trout.

It was a magical, spooky hour, and when I struck too hard and broke off my fly in the mouth of a fish that might have been even larger than the others, it ended quite abruptly. I groped my blind way to shore and found a boulder to sit upon. Then I closed my eyes and lifted my face toward the sky and allowed my senses to gluttonize on the sounds and smells of the dark river. I might have sat there for five minutes. Maybe it was an hour. Even my sense of time had been distorted by the night.

And I recalled some lines from Walt Whitman that I had once memorized optimistically—but, as it turned out, futilely—for the benefit of a blonde sophomore, with, I readily confess, seductive intent:

> I am he that walks with the tender and growing night,
> I call to the earth and sea half-held by the night.
> Press close bare-bosomed night—press close magnetic
>   nourishing night!
> Night of south winds—night of the large few stars!
> Still nodding night—mad naked summer night.

I've learned a few things about trout rivers in the nighttime since that eerie experience on the Connecticut River many years ago. But in many ways, nothing has changed. The big trout still like to come out to play in the dark of an August moon, and I still want to be there, eager to suspend my sense of sight in order to savor the sounds and smells, and to cast flies blindly, but not without purpose, to those trout. I confess to seductive intent.

I've fished moonless nights for striped bass off beaches, and I've drifted from midnight till dawn on bass ponds, and they are magical, too. But not as magical as a trout stream in the dark.

I've learned, for one thing, that in rivers large and small, east and west, the largest trout are generally most vulnerable after dark. Especially in the summer, they snooze in undiscoverable hiding places during the heat of the day, but they are energized by the descent of darkness. They have learned that the birds and mammals that prey upon them operate by sight and have the advantage in daylight. They have survived and grown large precisely because they have learned this. But they must eat. The safety of the darkness, plus cooling water temperatures, starts them feeding. At night these most cautious of trout cruise shallows boldly, secure in the knowledge that their predators have retired.

They don't expect to encounter human predators with fly rods. They are vulnerable to a Whitman-quoter with seduction in mind.

But the fisherman must stalk his nocturnal quarry with the same cunning as a daytime heron. I generally select a single pool for the evening, and pick the best place to stand in it, in the daylight. I move around as little as possible. For although at night an alligator brown trout might boldly chase baitfish or bugs in water barely deep enough to cover his dorsal, he remains the same wary, survival-tuned creature he is in the day. The crunching of gravel under a wader boot or an unnatural ripple rolling over smooth water will send him scooting back to bed for the night.

During the spinner falls that often begin at dusk and extend well into a summer's evening, these nocturnal feeders can be very selective. Fine leaders, drag-free floats, and delicate casting are just as important as they are under a midday sun. Precise fly imitation, in my experience, is less vital, although I try to match the size and the spent-wing silhouette of the actual insects during an after-dark spinner fall.

Many aquatic insects hatch after the sun leaves the water. A variety of mayflies, many of them large, come out at night. Several species of caddis begin to swarm predictably at nightfall. Darkness is the time when stone flies move on the surface of the river. When these delectables are on the water and big trout are marauding, I've found that a generic floater usually works fine. A Wulff or Humpy of the same approximate size as the natural insect will generally take fish. I cut my leader back to six or seven feet and tip it with two feet of 3X under these conditions.

Sometimes nothing particular is on the water, but the nocturnal cruisers are still feeding. They prowl the shallows, ready to gobble any wayward moth or beetle or hopper they come upon. I like to throw large bushy floaters—big hairwings or bivisibles that should be called lures rather than flies—in the direction of sloshing noises. Big trout attack them with the same heart-stopping explosion as a largemouth bass hitting one of Tap's deer-hair bugs.

Probably the best chance any of us will have to catch the biggest trout of our lives comes from casting big streamers into the darkness. For while the monsters we seek sometimes suck insects off the surface at night as they won't during the day-time, they remain primarily carnivores. They seek a nourishing mouthful, and they get it from baitfish, leeches, crawfish, mice, frogs, and juveniles of their own species. I like to use a floating line with a short, stout leader. Then I can fish the shallows and, if I want to probe deep pools, I can switch to a weighted fly without changing lines. Woolly Buggers and Gartside soft hackles tied on size six or eight streamer hooks convince trout that they're getting a meal in one bite. I twitch them slowly through pools, cast them across and let them swing through current lines, and strip them fast through the shallows—and I hang on.

No river is as gentle and amiable at night as it is during the daylight. The boulder you step over or around when you can see it will trip you up at night—at best filling your waders and sending you home prematurely, and at worst spilling you into currents that can drown you. All rivers have potholes, dropoffs, sunken logs, and other treacheries ready to waylay the unprepared fisherman.

It's not manly to venture into a river at night unprepared. It's simply stupid.

I live by four rules when I go night fishing on a trout river:

First, I never venture into unfamiliar water. I scout my river until I know what pool I want to spend the evening in. I use daylight to decide exactly where I will make my stand in that pool and how much I can move around. I pick a spot I can wade to and from safely. I look for overhanging branches and bushes fore and aft and for obstructions in the river such as rocks and fallen trees that can snag a miscast fly. I try to forecast where the trout will lie. I study my chosen pool until I have memorized all of its hazards, as well as its most likely hot spots, and can see them when I close my eyes.

Second, I never go fishing alone after dark. I bring a like-minded nighttime adventurer for both companionship and safety. We agree to fish within earshot of each other, which is rarely hard to arrange, since even the most heavily fished rivers are usually abandoned once the sun has set, and we can usually share the same pool. Sound carries well at night. Quiet conversation in the dark is pleasant, and it's comforting to know that someone is nearby to hear a call for help.

Third, I always wear an inflatable vest, for the obvious reason.

And, fourth (I'm embarrassed to admit how long it took for me to figure this out), I bring a flashlight. I love the darkness, and I like to activate the senses of touch and sound that remain dormant when I'm fishing in the daylight. But I like to know that I can see if I need to. I try not to shine my light on the water. But being able to see the path that winds through the woods to and from the river is, literally, better than a stick in the eye.

There are other items I've added to my daytime fishing vest for night work: a small clip-on light for fly changing and leader tying, an extra sweater for the night air that always grows cooler than expected, and waterproof matches, for the one time I'll want to dry off after an untimely drenching.

Since that evening thirty years ago on the Connecticut River, I've become addicted to casting flies into the darkness. Sometimes I fish trout rivers at night by design, and sometimes I just cannot drag myself away after the sun goes down. I've cast black caddis imitations onto the inky surface of the Bighorn under an inflated Montana moon. I've stayed with Hendrickson spinnerfalls on Connecticut's Farmington while night has descended and the frigid April air has numbed my fingers. I've lobbed Woolly Buggers against the banks of the Bow and the Green and the Missouri while my guides have magically maneuvered their driftboats through the darkness.

Sometimes I've caught the biggest fish of the day this way. Sometimes I've caught nothing. But I've never failed to savor the sensual pleasures and black mysteries of a trout river on a bare-bosomed mad naked summer night.

18

Deep-Freeze Trout

In my part of New England we call it the "January thaw." Leaden skies turn blue, the sun glows so bright it hurts your eyes, and snowbanks visibly shrink as the temperature climbs up through the forties. Snowmelt sends miniature trout streams trickling down roadsides. You can almost see the sap trying to rise in the maples.

Some years, the January thaw doesn't last more than a day or two. Some years it doesn't happen in January.

Some years, it doesn't happen at all.

But when it does happen, I find my own sap rising. The warm air awakens the urge that has lain as dormant as a winter trout in me. I must go fishing.

I don't believe that fishermen think like trout, and I'm certain that trout don't think like fishermen. It's doubtful that trout think at all, and there's plenty of evidence that fishermen don't, either.

But it does seem to be true that a fisherman's urge to go fishing coincides with a trout's urge to eat. The rule of thumb holds that trout bite best during the best time of day: midday during the cool months of spring and fall, early morning and after dark during summer's dog days.

The same fortuitous principle applies to winter trout: The days when you most feel like going fishing are generally the days when trout are most likely to feel like eating.

Cold-blooded creatures that trout are, their moods swing with their body temperature, which, of course, depends on the temperature of the water around them. They like it best around sixty degrees, and they can comfortably tolerate eight or ten degrees on either side. Under fifty and they begin to grow sulky and lethargic. Much above eighty and they die.

But like anglers, trout perk up when the temperature of their environment moves in a positive direction toward their comfort zone, even if it never gets there. If they've been simmering in seventy-eight-degree water for a couple of August weeks, the cold rain that drops the water temperature to seventy-four will spark a feeding frenzy. Likewise, a few days of false spring in January can cause stream temperatures to climb from thirty-eight into the low forties—still frigid in absolute terms, but, to trout, comparatively tropical.

I know one fisherman who disregards the weather and fishes for trout all winter. He doesn't mind knocking ice out of his guides every five minutes. He doesn't mind the layers of thermal clothing, the neoprene waders, or the woolen cap and gloves he must wear to prevent instant hypothermia.

Ed would rather be outdoors than indoors any time, and he'd rather try to catch a trout on a fly than do anything else. He relishes the solitude he finds on the same waters where, in May, fishermen jostle each other for elbow room. He takes frequent timeouts for a streamside fire and a mug of hot coffee, and if there's another fisherman around, he shares.

I suspect that what Ed likes best about it is how good it feels when he stops, although he will not admit it.

The weatherman promised southerly breezes, sunny skies, and temperatures climbing into the fifties. We hadn't had a fifty-degree day for two months. Tomorrow, I vowed, I go fishing.

The weatherman was wrong. In the morning, the red stuff in the thermometer stood about an inch tall.

I went fishing anyway.

He was standing in water up to his knees at the head of the pool when I got there. On the bank beside him a fire smoldered against a boulder. He wore polarized sunglasses and a fur-lined cap with earflaps fastened under his chin. I watched him for several minutes while I screwed up the courage to wade into the icy water. He seemed to have picked out a small area to fish, because he never moved. He was fishing a short line, casting upstream, following the drift with his rod tip, staring hard into the water, lifting, lobbing, over and over again.

As I watched, he suddenly raised his rod. It bowed momentarily, then went limp. I heard him grunt. He stripped in his fly, examined it, then cast it out again.

That was enough for me. I waded in a comfortable distance downstream from him and began to lob a brace of bushy weighted nymphs into the slow currents. I soon lost myself in the creaky rhythms of it.

Nothing happened except that my legs went numb.

After fifteen minutes I glanced up to see how the stranger upstream was doing. I spotted him crouched on the bank, warming his hands over his fire. He waved to me and held up a coffee mug. I needed no further invitation.

His face was creased and sun-fried. White stubble bristled on his chin. He said his name was Ed. He came here just about every day. He hardly ever saw another fisherman.

"There was supposed to be a January thaw today," I confessed. "Otherwise I probably wouldn't have come."

He nodded. "Those are the best days. But I figure, any day a man can go fishing is a good day, and at my age every day is a gift."

"You actually catch fish?"

He smiled. "Oh, sure. Some days are better than others. You've got to know where to find them, of course, and they're too cold to put up much of a tussle when you hook one. But, yes, I catch some. I catch a trout or two just about every day."

Ed's fire and his coffee and his enthusiasm warmed my bones, and he seemed grateful for my company. Every few minutes he thrust a piece of dead pine into the fire.

"There are three secrets to winter trout fishing," he told me. "One, you've got to know where to find them. Two, you've got to get them to bite. And three, you've got to know how to enjoy it. It's all different in the winter."

I nodded. None of this struck me as a great revelation, but I knew better than to interrupt. I figured Ed would impart some wisdom if I was patient. Besides, as long as he kept talking I had an excuse to huddle next to his fire.

When water temperatures plummet, he explained, trout tend to become concentrated in places that are marginally more comfortable for them. You won't find winter trout scattered the way you do in June. Most of the water is barren. But if you can find those warm spots—even a few degrees make all the difference— you'll find trout. Spring holes are best, he said, just as they are in midsummer, which is when he scouts them out. Spring water flows from the ground at constant temperatures year-round— cooler than the surrounding water in the summer, and warmer in the winter.

Tailwaters—rivers that are fed from the bottom of a dam— usually hold up better in the winter than freestone streams. The fish tend to congregate near the inflow, because as the water moves downstream, the frigid winter air rapidly cools it down.

Deep, slow-moving pools normally produce best in the absence of springs or tailwaters, for the same reason: Trout are most comfortable there. For winter trouting, a stream thermometer is as essential as a warm hat. Find the warmest water in the stream, and that's where you'll find fish.

Winter trout rarely feed enthusiastically. With their sluggish metabolisms, they expend little energy and require few calories. You can't expect them to chase and slash at your fly. But they will eat if something appetizing drifts to their mouths.

"Patience, of course," Ed said. "If you know the trout are there—and the best way to do that is to actually see them—then you've just got to keep at it. I always try to find visible trout. With a good pair of polarized glasses it's not hard. The water's normally low and clear in the winter, and you can wade quite close to the fish. They aren't very spooky in the winter. They don't like to leave their comfortable lies, and they don't have the energy to go scurrying away."

I showed Ed the pair of nymphs I had been using. "I didn't know what to tie on," I said.

He shrugged. "Usually pattern doesn't make much of a difference. I like to use neon pink and orange and chartreuse globugs—you know, egg patterns. Not that I think the fish particularly want to eat eggs, but I do think they are attracted to—or irritated by—the bright colors. Mainly, though, I like glo-bugs because I can see them in the water. I can see exactly where they are drifting in relation to the fish, which helps me to adjust the angle of my cast and the amount of lead I pinch onto my leader. I usually use two flies: sometimes two glo-bugs of different colors, sometimes one glo-bug for visibility and one nymph."

In the absence of visible fish, Ed said, he liked to crawl a black or olive woolly worm across the bottom of one of those deep slow pools that his thermometer suggested might harbor winter trout. "Right on the bottom," he emphasized. "Barely move it. I like to twitch it, let it sink all the way down, and let it rest there for a few seconds. Trout'll pick it up when it's falling. Sometimes they'll take it when it's lying there, not moving at all. Whether it's a nymph or a glo-bug or a woolly worm, you've got to be alert for the take, because these poor half-frozen critters don't do much more than open their mouths when they eat. The slightest hesitation in your leader and you've got to set your hook. If you can't see your fish and your fly, it's a good idea to use a strike indicator. More coffee?"

I held out my mug for a refill. "So it's all deep and slow stuff in the winter, huh?" I said.

He shrugged. "Usually. Some days you get a hatch. Midges'll come off almost any day the air temperature creeps up over forty. One of those bluebird days that you like, you can count on some midges. Whether or not the trout come up to them is another question, and I can't answer it for you except to say sometimes they do and sometimes they don't—which is one of the things I love about trout. There's winter caddis, too. Stream I know in Connecticut, tiny little caddis flies sometimes hatch even on the real cold days. I like to cast right up onto the shell ice and twitch the fly into the water. Those trout lie tight against the ice. Their little noses poke up within an inch of it. I've had good dry-fly fishing to that caddis hatch on days when my reel froze up solid."

We sat quietly for a few minutes sipping our coffee and gazing at the water. Ed's little fire had died to a few smoldering embers. I sensed that he was about to wade back into the stream. "You've told me how to find them and how to get them to bite," I said. "Didn't you say there was a third thing . . . ?"

He grinned. "Enjoying it. The third thing is knowing how to like it. You're young and smart. You prefer the warm days. So do I. So do the trout, for that matter. But even then it's tough. If you want fast fishing, if you want your trout to tear line off your reel—hell, if you want to be comfortable—if that's what you enjoy about fishing, wait till June. Fishin's always tough in the winter. And when you do manage to hook one of them, he gives you a fight like a hunk of frozen driftwood. You've got to dress for it. Neoprene waders, wool socks, thermal long johns, plenty of layers on top, woolen gloves, and most important of all, a warm hat." He stood up, fastened the flaps of his cap under his chin, and picked up his rod. "But if you're a nutty old codger like me, you like it tough. It reminds you that you're still alive."

I try it Ed's way a few times each winter—just to verify that I'm still alive. I shiver in knee-deep water and knock ice from my guides, allotting myself fifteen minutes between trips to my bankside fire. Now and then I even catch a few trout. Glo-bugs work on even the coldest winter days when I've managed to locate some trout clustered in a spring hole.

A trout river in the dead of winter can be a desolately beautiful black-and-white place—all dark ice and gray snow and black water and bare, gnarly trees. The fisherman feels that he and maybe a few distant crows are the only living things around—no warblers in the bushes, no insects in the air, no other fishermen in the water. Snowflakes spit from low pewter skies. Trout sulk on the bottom. It's a test for the spirit and bitter but nourishing medicine for the soul.

Deep-Freeze Trout

187

I still look forward to that January thaw, though. I'm not as tough as old Ed, I know, because even on those fair days, the best part comes when I stop.

19

Tailwaters

The most spectacular mayfly hatch I've ever seen happened on the Farmington River in Connecticut one misty May morning a few years ago. The Hendricksons made a layer of glimmering gray mist that blanketed the Beaver Pool, and hundreds of trout came to the surface to gorge on them. So many of the little smoky-winged sailboats drifted on the water that it was impossible to interest a trout in my lonely imitation. But it was a thrilling sight, and after a few minutes of frustration I reeled in and sat on a boulder, quite content to be there to witness it.

I took my first twenty-inch trout on a dry fly from Vermont's Lamoille River when I was a young teenager. We found him toward dusk feeding steadily at the tailout of a pretty pool, and he sucked in my Light Cahill on its first drift. The heaviest trout I've ever landed clanged Andy's eight-pound scale to the bottom. I'd spotted the crimson slash behind a boulder on Colorado's Frying Pan River fifty yards downstream from the Reudi Dam, and he engulfed the pink marabou shrimp fly I drifted onto his nose. That rainbow was a couple of pounds bigger than the one I took from the San Juan River in New Mexico, although the San Juan fish remains memorable because it ate a size twenty-two midge pupa that I'd tied to a 6X tippet.

The boulder-strewn Cheesman Canyon section of the South Platte River, also in Colorado, ranks as the prettiest trout stream I've ever fished, one notch above Utah's spectacular Green River in the Flaming Gorge. The Green, on the other hand, was the scene of the single greatest day of dry-fly fishing in my life. Andy and I lost count of the number of big trout we caught and released on cicada imitations that June day, but Mike Howard, our normally laconic guide, called it "awesome and disgusting."

The Swift River in central Massachusetts boasts neither gorgeous scenery nor profuse hatches. But it's my home water, and I've caught trout every month of the year from the Swift, which makes it special to me.

Taking everything into consideration, however—wild beauty, dependable long-season dry-fly action, predictable hatches, abundant big trout, and a lifetime of memories—my favorite trout river of all is Montana's Bighorn. It's no coincidence that every one of these rivers is a tailwater.

Hydroelectric and flood-control dams have inundated forests, destroyed ecosystems, buried villages, and blocked the spawning migrations of anadromous fish. My father, a devout Atlantic salmon angler, regularly and enthusiastically cussed out the dam-builders and the concrete-and-steel monstrosities they built. When he growled the words "Army Corps of Engineers," you might have thought he had said "serial killers."

But for every quid there is a quo. The rivers that flow from those dams make ideal trout water. Find a tailwater, and odds are you'll find the best and most dependable trout fishing in the area. That why when we EMSPPMDJDFDA (Eastern Massachusetts Stud Poker, Pale Morning Dun, Jack Daniel's, Freudian Dream Analysts) set off on our annual Columbus Day Weekend–Trout Bombing Mission, we always head to a tailwater. We have never failed to catch some large trout, regardless of the weather. We've always found them eating midges, and on a gray

October afternoon, blue-winged olives usually bring them to the surface.

A tailwater, by definition, is a river that is fed from reservoir water that flows from the bottom of a dam. As spring moves into summer, the water in reservoirs stratifies. Water is heaviest at thirty-nine degrees, so it sinks to the bottom, where it stays. This cold bottom layer (which is called the hypolimnion—I looked it up) is insulated from the warm top layer (epilimnion) by the thin middle layer (thermocline). Sediment settles to the bottom of the reservoir, while vegetation decomposes in the hypolimnion. The water that feeds the river is clear, cold, and rich in nutrients, ideal for trout and other aquatic life.

Because the water near the bottom of a reservoir is always cool, the first ten or twelve miles of a tailwater flow at constant year-round temperatures, typically between fifty and sixty degrees—which happens to be smack in the trout's comfort zone.

Certain species of aquatic insects, scuds, and other trout forage thrive in this temperature zone, too. Midges, blue-winged olives, pale morning duns, Tricos, sulphurs, some drakes, and a few species of caddisflies, along with a seasonal mix of terrestrials, are typical tailwater fare. Because of the narrow range of water temperatures, on the other hand, large stone flies and many other common species of aquatic insects, whose life cycles apparently depend on fluctuating water temperatures, are generally scarce in tailwaters.

But what tailwaters might lack in variety of insect hatches, they more than compensate for in abundance and predictability. Tailwater bugs typically emerge like clockwork and in breathtaking numbers, and the same hatches frequently continue, day after day, every day, for a month or more. You can mark your calendar and plan your trip months ahead of time, confident that you'll hit the tailwater hatch on schedule.

The angler who grooves on solving the arcane mysteries of matching compound-complex hatches might find a tailwater disappointing. It's usually pretty easy to figure out what the trout are eating, because typically only one insect hatches at a time. Even when there is no surface activity, the angler can always catch fish by matching the nymph of the insect that's scheduled to emerge. When in doubt, midge larvae and pupae drifted near the bottom always work.

In undammed freestone rivers, trout tend to become lethargic as water temperatures rise in the summer and again when they plummet in the winter. Insect hatches are seasonal, brief, sparse, and unpredictable. Freestoners generally fish best in the spring and the fall, when water levels and temperatures are optimal, but early (or late) runoff, drought, flash flood, and heat wave can spoil the fishing.

Tailwaters are unaffected by such variables, so their trout remain active, and can be caught, throughout the year. And because they never stop feeding, they grow faster—and are more abundant—than their freestone counterparts. Measured in pounds of trout per river mile, the Green and the Bighorn ranked one and two in the country the last time I looked. The world record brown trout (it weighed over forty pounds) came from the Greers Ferry tailwater in Arkansas.

A few years ago, when the turbines at the Reudi Dam were chopping up mysis shrimp and spitting the pieces into the Frying Pan, the trout ate so well that they became as fat and piggy as rugby balls. Biologists determined that there were one thousand pounds of trout per surface acre in the upper reaches of the Frying Pan in those days. It was, of course, a weird, unexpected, and aberrant situation—the sort of thing that can only happen on a tailwater.

The ecology of tailwaters is not yet fully understood. Compared to natural rivers, tailwaters are newborn infants. We don't have much history to help us understand how they grow and change. Every dam has its purpose—flood control, power generation, drinking water, irrigation—and no one has figured out how various water-release schedules affect a tailwater's trout and aquatic insects. The once-prolific pale morning duns have all but disappeared from the Bighorn in recent years, for example, and nobody can explain why or predict when or if they will return.

On some tailwaters, flows are regulated and moderated for the benefit of the fishing. On others, the commercial purpose of the dam comes before the well-being of the river's trout. Water may be held back until the river shrinks to a deadly trickle, or it may be released suddenly and unpredictably and in great volume. The river can flood in a matter of minutes, which disorients its trout and scours its bed, dislodging weeds and insects and destroying spawning areas.

It also can drown an unwary angler. Since the day a surging wall of water nearly killed me on the Deerfield in western Massachusetts, I have never fished a tailwater without checking the release schedule and remaining alert to changes in the water level. When the gurgle of the river deepens into a roar, I get out first and ask questions later.

Like my father, I sometimes curse the dam-builders. I'm always saddened and angered by the ugliness of a giant concrete structure looming over what had once been a beautiful, unspoiled wilderness and a wild river. But short of dynamite, the best revenge I know is to wade around the corner, put the dam out of sight, and catch some big trout.

20

The Keeper Quest

The June sun had not yet cracked the horizon. A layer of fog shrouded the masts of the moored sailboats. Art Currier steered slowly through the harbor of the Merrimack River in Newburyport, heading out toward Plum Island where, we had heard, the blues had started to appear. We wanted to catch some on the fly rod.

My nine-weight was rigged with a big white Deceiver and eight inches of wire shock tippet. I stood up in the bow, watching the water, but it was Art who saw the birds first, dozens of terns and gulls wheeling and diving in the fog.

He gunned it, then cut the engine, and we drifted into casting range. My line was already in the air.

The panicky baitfish were silvering at the surface, sometimes leaping all the way out of the water, and beneath them I could see the flashes of slashing predatory fish.

My fly landed a little short. I began stripping. Almost instantly it stopped. I hauled back, driving home the hook. From behind me I heard Art grunt. I turned my head. His rod was arced.

"I dunno," he muttered. "Doesn't feel like a blue."

It wasn't. A few minutes later, each of us landed a striped bass. They were twins, a shade under twenty inches long.

"Schoolies," said Art. "I'll be damned."

We released them hastily, cast toward the school, and hooked up again.

By the time we landed those fish, the birds had followed the tide a hundred yards downriver. While Art fired up the engine, I clipped off my wire tippet and tied on a popper. A few minutes later Art and I were doubled up again.

We chased that school of stripers for more than an hour before we lost them. We figured we'd landed more than a dozen fish apiece, and every one of them was within an inch of twenty.

We fished hard for the rest of the morning and never had a strike.

That happened seven or eight years ago, and although I grew up in New England and have squandered most of my life on the water, until that morning on the Merrimack I'd never caught a striped bass on a fly.

Since then I've caught hundreds. Thanks to some nick-of-time restrictions on both sport and commercial fishing, Northeast striped bass populations have rebounded from near extinction. Now schools of linesides swarm our beaches, rocks, jetties, estuaries, and tidal rivers from April through October.

Casting flies for stripers may be the fastest-growing sport along the Northeast coast. Saltwater veterans are putting away their spinning gear and taking up fly rods. Trout fishermen are investing in ten-weight outfits. Deep-sea guides have stowed their bluewater charts, trolling rods, and electronic fish-finders to explore inshore waters. Everyone is discovering that stripers eat flies and pull hard.

The fly rod makes good conservation sense, too. A single—preferably barbless—hook permits the safe release of what will be predominantly undersized fish (if a thirty-two-inch fish can possibly be called "undersized"). Nobody wants to put back a striper that's swallowed a bait or been mangled by treble hooks.

The new regulations have given me what is, admittedly, an arbitrary goal: I want to catch a "keeper" on a fly. A keeper, I believe, defines a big striper.

Under the first Massachusetts regs, any striper under thirty-six inches had to be returned. In those years I landed several that measured between thirty-two inches and thirty-four inches.

Then they reduced the definition of a big bass to thirty-four inches. Now I can't seem to land one over thirty inches.

Schoolies are great fun on a fly rod, and I never tire of catching them. But it seems that all the saltwater fly rodders I know speak matter-of-factly of the keepers they've taken. "You just gotta be in the right place at the right time with the right fly," they shrug.

I am grateful for their wisdom. Very instructive.

My quest for a keeper is becoming an obsession. I just want to catch one. I don't plan to keep it.

The other morning at the hardware store, my town's fishing sage (every New England town has at least one self-appointed fishing sage) told me that he'd been catching lots of stripers. A keeper or two almost every time out, he said with a shrug.

"Where," I asked casually, "are you finding them?"

He jerked his thumb over his shoulder, in an easterly direction. "The ocean," he said. "It's full of 'em."

Which, of course, was about as helpful as the advice I got one October from a New Hampshire game warden. I told him that my old reliable woodcock covers had been coming up pretty empty, and I sure could use a little guidance from a wise person who spent his life in the woods. He puffed thoughtfully on his pipe for a moment, gazed up at the sky, then tilted his head to me. "Woodcock," he whispered conspiratorially, "are where you find 'em."

If you want to figure out how to catch striped bass on a fly rod, there's no substitute for spending a lot of time on the water. Except there's an awful lot of water in the ocean, and deciphering it would take more time than I have.

Even learning a tiny piece of it is a full-time job. The fact is, regardless of how abundant the stripers are, you can't cast randomly into the ocean and expect to catch any. There are plenty of "right places," but there are an infinitely greater number of wrong ones.

The right places, moreover, are constantly changing. Stripers are always on the move, and to figure out where and when you can intercept them requires factoring a mind-numbing array of variables: time of day or night, phase of moon, tide, wind, season, weather, depth, structure, and "hatches" and movement of bait. I know I've forgotten some of them.

Even when you get it all right, you've still got to be lucky.

Because the combinations of variables shift continually, what you figured out yesterday won't necessarily help you today, as Phil Craig and I discovered one night on Martha's Vineyard. We'd done our homework, and at sunset we were stationed on the jetty by the bridge where a strong ebbing tide was washing bait out of the pond. It was, according to all the locals (many of whom were there with us), the current hot spot, the place to hang a keeper on a fly.

We cast into the darkness until the tide turned without a strike.

"We slaughtered 'em at Lobsterville," we kept hearing the next day. "On that wind, you gotta be over on that side of the island."

Oh.

Phil and I did find fish sucking in cinderworms one evening on Tashmoo Pond. Their slurps sounded like toilets flushing. Some of the swirls we saw could have been made by keepers. We learned that stripers can be as selective as brown trout when they're eating cinderworms.

Tony Biski specializes in wade-fishing for stripers on the sand flats off Chatham. It's all sight fishing. Bonefish stuff. Throw Clousers into the paths of cruising fish and hang on. Keepers? Sure.

Except the day Andy Gill and I were there a heavy cloud cover and stiff wind ruined the visibility. We couldn't cast to what we couldn't see.

From Mike Hintlian's boat Andy and I heaved big Whistlers on shooting heads into the surf breaking against the rocky cliffs around Rockport and Gloucester. The bass lay with their noses facing the rocks, taking the bait that washed back to them.

"You want a keeper," said Mike, "meet me at midnight."

We did. Except ten-foot seas, gale-force winds, and driving rain prevented us from taking the boat out of the harbor.

In April Phil Farnsworth showed us how to read the rips along the Connecticut beaches, and when we drifted our flies just right we found schoolies. Phil showed me how to use a stripping basket and a two-handed retrieve.

The keepers, he said, wouldn't show up for a month or two.

I met Rip Cunningham before the magic hour on a June morning to prowl one of the complex estuary systems on the Massachusetts south shore. Rip knows where to find stripers under every combination of variables in this little corner of the Atlantic Ocean. On the incoming tide, Rip climbed onto his platform and poled me across sand flats, and we saw what he swore were thirty-pounders. Unfortunately, by the time we spotted them in the glare they were scooting.

We caught fourteen-inch schoolies and thirty-two-inch brutes from rips, channels, and structure, and then I hooked one that felt bigger by another dimension than any of them. It took me into my backing, turned, and raced back past the stern.

When Rip glimpsed it, he whistled. "Big fish," he whispered.

A minute later my line went limp. I reeled in and saw what I expected: a pigtail at the end of my leader instead of a fly.

"Bad knot," I observed needlessly.

"Too bad," said Rip. "That one was definitely a keeper."

Keith Wegener and I have followed tide and bait and rumor all over Casco Bay and the mouth of the Kennebec. We've found stripers crashing menhaden against the rocks and swarming over mudflats and holing up in creeks.

Other days we've fished the same places at the same tides with the same flies and come home skunked.

Time on the water, I know. I just don't have enough of it.

Stripers have obsessed me for several years now. I'll take 'em, whatever size they're running. I do not sneer at schoolies. I love the variety. They suck in hatching cinderworms like trout taking mayfly emergers. They cruise mussel beds and mud and sand flats, making "nervous water" and sometimes tailing like bonefish. They look like tarpon ghosting under the surface. I've caught them on top with poppers and from deep holes with fast-sinking lines and lead-eyed flies. I've caught them from tiny tidal creeks and from breaking surf. I've caught them at all times of day and night, from early spring to late fall.

Stripers at various times eat sand eels, shrimp, crabs, spearing, and herring, and you need trout-sized flies that closely imitate those baits to catch them. When they're chasing bunker or squid, it takes a fly as big as your foot to fool them.

Of course, sometimes they'll strike anything you throw at them.

I've been in the wrong place plenty of times. When I've managed to be at the right place at the right time with the right fly, it's always because I've been taken there by someone who knows more than I do.

So far, that keeper has eluded me. But I've learned one thing: The most efficient way to find stripers is to accept an invitation from somebody who spends a lot of time on the water.

V

Why They Call It Fishing, Not Catching

Sir Henry Wotton . . . was a most dear lover, and a frequent practicer of the art of angling; of which he would say, "it was an employment for his idle time, which was then not idly spent . . . a rest to his mind, a cheerer of his spirits, a diverter of sadness, a calmer of unquiet thoughts, a moderator of passions, a procurer of contentedness; and that it begat habits of peace and patience in those that professed and practiced it."

—Izaak Walton, *The Compleat Angler*

21

A Bridge Too Near

The little brook with the Indian name rises in springs deep in a swamp, meanders through woods and bog and marsh and meadow, parallels the old Boston & Maine railbed for a mile or so, passes beneath several secondary roads and one state highway, slips behind a shopping mall and a Ford dealership, joins another brook similar to it, and empties into a larger river that eventually makes its way to the Atlantic Ocean.

If the office building across the street weren't in the way, I could see the brook from my third-floor front window. I guess it's as close to home water as I have. My home run, you might say.

By a well-traveled trout fisherman's standards it's not much of a brook, although the state stocks it with brown trout every spring and a few of them find sanctuary in springholes where they manage to survive and grow for a few seasons. The largest trout I've ever taken from my brook measured sixteen inches. He ate a size twenty-two black ant at 5:30 one August morning, and he was the only trout I saw that day.

I broke off a bigger one that hit a Marabou Muddler the day after a September nor'easter had blown through. I saw the gold flash of his flank and felt his strength and, at least in my memory, he matched the twenty-inchers I've caught in Montana.

When I fish my brook, it's because the impulse of the moment is too powerful to resist. I must go fishing then, and I don't have time to travel to more compelling places. So I drive the familiar back roads and park my car in hidden places and trek over hills and slog through swamps to pools that I fancy I alone know about. If I find a tangle of monofilament or a beer can at one of these secret holes, I stop going there. I value the illusion that a few parts of the brook belong only to me, and when I fish in it I cast for solitude as well as brown trout.

The road to the post office crosses my brook at a stone bridge a scant half mile from my house. A rocky riffle flows out of the woods and under the bridge, and on the downstream side a delicious pool opens up. Hatchery trucks make regular stops here, as do gangs of fishermen who harbor no illusions and do not value solitude. Tall trees and alders and briers and wild grapevines border the pool, but years of fishermen have trampled paths along the banks and cut openings to the water big enough for a man with a spinning rod to heave out a red-and-white plastic bobber.

Because I visit the post office virtually every day, and because I am constitutionally unable to drive past moving water without stopping, I fish here regularly, and I have for years.

I fish, that is, mentally. The bridge pool is too well known and too lacking in solitude to appeal to me. I leave my gear in the car, slip on my polarized glasses, and lean my elbows on the bridge rail. I look for rising trout and hatching insects, and even when I see none I sometimes spot a heron or a kingfisher or a mink hunting along the edges.

Often there are human fishermen there. Mostly they are slinging spinning lures or dredging the bottom with bait, and unless they're kids I don't bother talking to them, because after "Any luck?" we don't have anything to say to each other.

Sometimes, though, I'll find a fly fishermen casting in the bridge pool. Then, from my spot at the rail, I kibitz and speculate about bugs and patterns and tippets.

Once, in April, I found a young guy casting diligently toward the swirls that pockmarked the surface of the pool. I watched him for a while. He changed flies often and never rose a fish. Finally I called to him: "Any luck?"

He turned, shaded his eyes, then shook his head. "Can't figure what they're taking. Tried everything."

"You sure they're trout?"

"Oh, yeah. Big browns."

Peering straight down into the water from my perch on the bridge, I could see the swarms of spawning suckers. Now and then one of them would lift from the bottom and roll at the surface, and they did flash the buttery yellow of a brown trout.

I watched the angler cast dry flies to those suckers for a while, then called, "Well, good luck," before I left.

The odd fact is this: I have never seen anyone actually catch a trout from this pool. I'm not saying it's never been done. But not when I've been watching.

By the beginning of June I rarely see fishermen in the bridge pool. So when the March Brown spinners fall at dusk, I have the place to myself. I take my post at the rail and watch the browns sip while swallows dart over the water and frogs grump from the edges and mosquitoes swarm thicker than the mayflies.

These fish, I know, would be easy, and I always wish there were a competent angler in the pool for me to watch. I've never had any desire to try it myself. Catching them in my mind is enough. Then one evening I stopped at the bridge just as darkness was settling over the pool. I took my customary place, leaned my forearms on the rail, and saw two men with spinning rods heaving bobbers amid the spinner-sipping trout. The heavy bobbers hit the water with a crash, but that didn't seem to deter the gorging trout, who just kept on feeding.

Clouds of spinners swarmed over the water, and at first it was amusing, knowing that those two guys had no chance whatsoever of catching a trout. But the longer I watched the more frustrated I became. It didn't seem fair. Those trout deserved better than spinning rods and nightcrawlers suspended under bobbers.

Finally I couldn't stand it. I decided to break my own rule and, for the first time ever, cast a fly into the bridge pool. I went back to my car, assembled my rod, and by the light of the dome tied on a size fourteen rusty spinner. I found an opening on the edge of the pool directly across from the two guys with spinning rods. They ignored me, but I knew they were watching me, and I was glad of it. I wanted to show them what a man with a fly rod and the right insect imitation would do. I was a fly-fishing evangelist. Maybe my example would convert these two guys. Rising trout deserved flies.

The trees behind me posed a tricky backcast challenge, but I managed a short cast to a sipper just upstream from one of the red-and-white bobbers. I mended my line and squinted into the gathering gloom at my fly. It drifted to the trout, which sucked it in as expected. I lifted my rod—just a hair too quickly and firmly. My line sailed back over my head into the trees and alders and briers. I tugged at it, but it was hopeless.

One of the guys across the pool said something. It sounded like, "Didya see that?"

I broke off the fly in the branches. My tippet stayed with it. My fly box and glasses and flashlight were still in the car. Darkness had seeped out of the woods and spilled onto the pool.

I reeled in and headed back. When I paused at the bridge rail, I heard the two spin-fishermen laughing.

The next night the March Brown spinners were again falling and the brown trout were sipping. I caught seven of them in the hour before dark without breaking off a single fly. I had the pool to myself the entire time.

After that, I continued to visit the pool almost every evening. The spinner fall petered out, of course. A few nights later I saw some green drakes on the water, and two or three trout were chasing them. Then came caddis. I left my rod in the car, but I caught many trout in my mind.

One July evening, long after I figured the bridge pool had become too warm and sluggish to harbor trout, I watched a heron catch his limit. He stood at the edge of the tailout, his head cocked and his eye intent on the water, and when he struck he never missed. He lifted his head with a fish wiggling in his beak every time. They looked like trout, although I couldn't be sure. I was tempted to rig up my rod and see if I could outfish the heron, but I didn't. I figured he'd laugh at me.

22

Beating the Bass Boats

Give me a glitter-painted torpedo-shaped bass boat with fifty
horses hung on the transom and a foot-operated battery-pow-
ered trolling motor up front. Perch me high on a padded swivel
seat, stick an eight-weight fly rod in my hand, let me read the
water off the screen of an electronic fish-finder, and I'll stuff as
many pounds of largemouth into the livewell as any stick-baitin'
pig-'n-jiggin' rubber-wormin' treble-hookin' lip-rippin' tournament bubba on the circuit.

I believe this. It might be fun to try to prove it sometime. It
could revolutionize an entire industry.

Scary, isn't it, the image of a fleet of high-tech fly fishermen
traveling the bass circuit in pursuit of cash prizes and chewing

tobacco endorsements and their own Saturday morning cable television shows?

No, wait. Please. Don't give me the boat. I don't want it. Give me a canoe or a float tube, if you like, though I'll be just as happy to roll up my pant legs and get wet. Above all, give me solitude. Let me wade or paddle along a quiet shoreline as the summer sun slips behind the hills. Give me targets to shoot at: half-submerged logs, overhanging bushes, openings in the weedbeds. Let me hear the soft pop and burble of my deerhair bug and the heart-stopping glug of a largemouth inhaling it.

I don't want to compete with anybody.

My hate-affair with bass boats began several years ago on Lake Winnipesaukee. After Dad retired to New Hampshire, he and I liked to paddle his seventeen-foot Grumman around the islands and along the boulder-studded shoreline casting bugs and streamers for smallmouths. Nobody except us had much interest in those bass. Rarely did we see other fishermen, and when we did, they were wire-line trolling out in the middle. Winnipesaukee was renowned for its landlocked salmon and lake trout. We had no problem sharing the big lake with those guys.

Then came the bass boats. They descended suddenly and all at once, like a blizzard hatch of caddis flies. They raked the shorelines with treble hooks, sometimes three men to a boat and a boat every hundred feet. When there wasn't a tournament going on, the spin-men were there anyway, practicing their high-tech tricks. They caught a lot of fish. Probably almost as many as Dad and I used to catch on the fly rod.

Before I knew it, the bass-boat armada was patroling the Charles and Sudbury rivers, my "home" bass waters in eastern Massachusetts where I had fly fished in relative peace since I was a kid. Most of my "secret" bass ponds got discovered. Bass boats swarmed anyplace a trailer could be backed into the water.

It kept happening this way: I'd slip my canoe or float tube into the water a couple of hours before sunset on a summer evening and start paddling. I'd move at a leisurely pace, working the shoreline along the way, trying to time it so that I'd turn the point into a particular dark cove about the time the bats and the nighthawks came out. That cove—all of my favorite bass places had such a cove—featured a fallen tree or two, sunken brush heaps, overhanging bushes, lily pads . . . and a few big bass eager to ambush a slowly twitched deerhair bug.

My anticipation built steadily as I paddled the shoreline. I usually caught some fish along the way. But it was the cove that lured me.

The first time I found a bass boat parked in my cove I wanted to yell: "Hey! This is my place. I discovered it twenty years ago. It just took me over an hour to paddle here. Now I've got no place to go except home."

I cursed through my teeth. But I yelled nothing, of course, and the guys up on their swivel seats didn't even notice me. They were too busy talking and laughing and casting spinnerbaits into my cove, ripping an occasional lip and generally having a helluva good time. Besides, I understood that getting there first was part of their competitive game, the justification for their speedboat with its fifty-horse motor. They'd won and I'd lost. That's what bass fishing had become.

After it had happened a few times, I realized that I no longer had any secret bass coves.

Sour grapes? You bet.

I never lost my love of fly casting for bass. The moment when a four-pound largemouth shatters the stillness of a soft summer evening, leaving a hole in the flat dark water where my bug had been twitching, remained vivid and magic in my memory.

But Dad and I quit paddling his Grumman on Winnipesaukee, and the only times I launched my float tube or canoe were to cast to midging trout on an April pond. I had no appetite for competing with the bass boats. Soon I quit fly fishing for bass altogether. I became a trout specialist.

The local brook with the Indian name—my "home" trout stream—flows low and warm and sluggish in the summer, and I usually stop fishing there when the first dry spell arrives in June. But several years ago a three-day July gullywasher brought the water level up more than a foot. From my vantage at the bridge rail, it looked like a trout stream again, and I couldn't resist the quixotic urge to give it a try.

So I drove to one of my secret pools, retrieved my seven-foot fly rod from the trunk, tied a brown Woolly Worm to the tippet, pulled on my hip boots, slogged through the wet woods, and slithered down the muddy slope. The currents were swirling and eddying around the boulders just the way they did in May when hatchery browns and brookies sipped Hendrickson spinners.

The brook trout, of course, had all turned belly-up by now, and as relatively hardy as they are, I doubted that any of the browns had survived the June drought, either.

Well, maybe one brown had made it. That's all I wanted.

I figured it was all pretend. But it was good to stand in my stream again with the little two-weight in my hand and the soft rain on my face, drifting that buggy nymph through the pool, and I quickly lost myself in the rhythms and memories of it.

The strike came hard and sudden and unexpected, and when I raised my rod and felt the muscular pull at the other end, I thought: *Yes! Big carryover brown trout. I'm a genius.*

Then my brown trout jumped, and it wasn't a brown. It wasn't even a trout.

It was a largemouth bass. About a three-pounder.

Nuts, I thought. *A damn bass. Some genius.*

It jumped again, rattling its gills, and when it hit the water it sent waves sloshing against both banks of the narrow pool. Then it surged downstream, heading for the tailout of my secret little pool in the woods. I gave it as much pressure as I dared. I feared for the 4X tippet. My little two-weight bent double.

By the time I managed to turn that bass and work it to my feet and pinch its lower lip between my thumb and forefinger and lift it from the water, I was thinking: Maybe I *am* a genius.

After I released the fish, I sat on a boulder to ponder it. My little trout stream meanders through swamp and marsh and woods, parallels the railroad tracks behind the strip mall, and passes under several highway bridges. A few smaller streams join it along the way before it finally empties into one of my formerly "secret" bass ponds, a place I quit fishing when the bass-boat army occupied it.

I doubted if that bass had retreated up into the stream to escape attacking spinner-baits. It had simply wandered away, searching for food and shelter and comfort, the way all fish do. To the bass, the little stream was part of its pond.

Where one bass lived, I figured, there likely would be others. Best of all, no bass boat could navigate this stream.

And so I began exploring my stream, and then other trout-sized streams, for summer bass. I studied topographic maps, looking for thin blue lines that connected, however indirectly, to known bass waters. I trekked through bogs and woods to check them out. Many of them proved to be dried-up streambeds or otherwise fishless. No prospector strikes gold with every swing of his pickaxe.

But enough of them held bass to revive my lust for bass fishing with the fly rod. I fished those little streams trout-style: drifting buggy nymphs, floating bushy dry flies, and twitching streamers with my seven-foot two-weight.

Gradually I widened my search. I hunted down waters that held bass—and were inaccessible to bass boats. Here's what I learned:

Bass live in virtually every little pothole pond in the Northeast. Before bulldozers moved earth to create highways and housing developments and shopping malls, most of these potholes were linked to the big rivers—the Merrimack, the Charles, and the Connecticut—that drain the New England hills. Those big rivers hold bass, and so do all waters presently or formerly connected to them. In fact, I've discovered that anyplace that looks "bassy," however small, probably *is* bassy.

Just about every pond and warmwater river and stream of any size, in fact, holds bass. I simply avoid those with trailer access. Cape Codders, for example, boast that they have as many ponds as there are days in the year, a forgivable exaggeration. Many of these glacier-formed "kettle-holes" hold trout; but virtually all of them (except those that have been reclaimed) hold bass. Enough of them are surrounded by private property or are otherwise off-limits to bass boats to attract a fly rodder in a float tube.

Many small New England towns used to dig water-holding pits for their local fire departments. Most of them cover an acre or less, but they are usually deep and spring-fed, and bass—sometimes surprisingly big ones—live in many of them.

Recreational canoeists, I've found, are happy to share their favorite destinations with anybody who curses gasoline motors. They've generously guided me to several quiet-water bass meccas.

The tributaries of bass rivers also hold bass. They tend to be winding and weedy and barricaded with fallen trees. While the torpedo boats patrol the main river, a man in a canoe can slink into water that is rarely fished. Likewise, tournament-minded bass fishermen usually stick to the main bodies of water, where they can decipher structure off their loran monitors. Often the inlets and outlets of bass lakes and ponds are navigable by canoe, and they're generally well populated with native bass.

I've even bribed groundskeepers at local golf courses into letting me cast bass bugs on their water hazards. This, I've found, can be hazardous indeed when foursomes are hitting from the tees. But it doesn't take many five-pound largemouths to make the risk acceptable.

I've ceded my old bass haunts to the high-tech boats. I refuse to compete with them. Lake Winnipesaukee, the Charles and Sudbury rivers, and a score of other ponds, lakes, and rivers that I used to haunt now belong to them.

But anyplace where they can't go is now mine. I've found a dozen secret new bass places within a twenty-minute drive of my house, places where I can wet-wade and catch largemouths on a trout rod or paddle my tube or canoe along a shaded evening shoreline and hear my deerhair bug gurgle when I twitch it past a fallen oak tree. They're all places where I know I won't find a bass boat parked in the cove around the point.

Don't ask me to show them to you. Go find your own. And if I find you parked in my favorite pool or cove some evening after I've slogged through the woods or paddled my tube along the shoreline to get there, I will, you can be sure, curse you through my teeth.

But I will concede: You won and I lost. I'll get you next time.

I guess bass fishing is always competitive.

23

A Slam for Taku

We waded the flats that first afternoon, and Taku spotted an enormous school of bonefish flashing and circling in the emerald-clear sunlit water. Now and then a fish rose to the glassy surface to feed like a brown trout sipping mayflies. Taku shook his head. "When the bones risin' like that," he said, "eet mean a change in the weather."

"What kind of change?"

"Wind comin'."

I gave him a skeptical smile.

"The bones, they no lie, mon," he said.

The next morning Andy and I awoke to the woody rattling of the palms outside our cabin. Coconuts banged off the roof like a mortar barrage. Dark clouds skidded across the low pewter sky. Out beyond the reef, whitecaps chopped the water, and when we sped off in Taku's skiff for the lagoons that lay inside the ring of the Turneffe Islands archipelago, we found even the sheltered flats gray and corrugated by the wind.

How would the conditions affect our chances for catching a permit?

"Good and bad, mon," shrugged Taku. "Hard for feesh to see us, good. Hard for us to see them, bad."

April and May are the best permit fishing months on the salt-water flats off the coast of Belize. Andy and I had come with the dream of catching one on a fly, which, by virtually universal consensus, is the ultimate fly-fishing achievement. Permit are spooky and wily and incredibly strong. They are taken on live bait—crabs are best—with fair regularity. But they strike flies reluctantly.

Landing a permit is the fly fisherman's no-hitter, hole-in-one, or 300 game. Pick your metaphor.

Taku had been guiding world-class flats fishermen such as George Anderson, Mike Lawson, and Winston Moore from the Turneffe Flats lodge since October. Three fly-caught permit had come into his boat this season.

He told us he was tied with Pops for the lead among the lodge's guides. "You gonna put me ahead of Pops, huh?" he said.

Andy and I smiled. Taku did not smile.

Andy took the casting deck first. Taku climbed up on his platform and poled us effortlessly through the persistent wind along the edges of dropoffs and shoals, and I learned the drill: Taku would suddenly yell, "Feesh!" and the fisherman would stare at the water and cry, "Where?"

"Eleven o'clock, mon! Queek!" And then, "He's gone. You gotta be queeker, mon. Them permit, they some spooky feesh."

Taku invariably saw them first. They traveled in singles and pairs, always moving, usually far from the boat, often in the wrong direction. If they were headed for us, Taku's voice took an extra edge of excitement. "Coming at us, mon! Twelve o'clock! Geeve it to heem!" And if you didn't see the fish, you had the choice of casting blindly—a waste of time—or not casting at all. Either way, you missed the chance.

And if you did see the fish—which is the first of many essential permit-fishing skills—you had to drop your crab fly, softly, six feet directly into his path and hope it would sink to his level when he got there, and that he wouldn't spook when he saw it.

Then you had to twitch it just right and let it drop back at the precise instant. If you did all of those things perfectly, and did them often enough, eventually a permit might try to eat your fly.

You have time for just one double-hauled cast in that wind— one backcast to get the fly line moving, and one hard, precise forward cast.

Catching permit on a fly rod used to be an accident. Then came serious efforts to construct a fly that looked and acted like a crab, which is virtually all that permit eat. Now crab flies are constructed from spun, clipped, and colored wool and deerhair, as well as a variety of synthetic materials. They are weighted to sink quickly. They are big and bulky and, even on a nine-weight rod, they are no fun to cast. Especially in the wind, and especially when you've got just one shot to drop it precisely six feet in front of a cruising permit.

Some fishermen impregnate their crab flies with the juices of real crabs. It's not altogether clear whether this is ethical or not, but Andy and I didn't do it.

Taku spotted seven or eight permit during Andy's hour on the casting deck. He cast to three or four of them. "Bad shot," Taku would grumble at an inaccurate cast, or, "You got to be *queek*, mon."

One permit turned and followed Andy's fly for a few feet before darting away. When he climbed down from the deck at the end of his hour, his eyes were sparkling. "I think I'm gonna have a heart attack," he said. "This is intense."

"Plenty of feesh today," remarked Taku. "Wind makes 'em move."

I stripped out line and braced myself on the rolling casting deck. I stared at the water. My polarized glasses did little to cut the reflected glare from the gray sky. I couldn't understand how anybody saw anything that was moving beneath the choppy surface, and when Taku yelled, "Feesh!" I looked wildly and saw nothing.

"Mon, he was right there."

"I couldn't see anything."

"You got to look, mon, or eet's no good."

"Sorry. I'm trying."

This was not relaxing sport.

We hunted permit every morning. Taku poled through the wind from his precarious platform high over the stern, while Andy and I took our one-hour turns on the deck in the bow. We stared hard into the dark wind-chopped water. Gradually we learned to recognize the anomalous dark shapes of cruising permit, and a couple of times Andy and I actually spotted a fish before Taku did. We got in some good shots, had a few follows, and Taku grudgingly admitted that we were catching on to it. "Yeah, maybe we catch one," he said after Andy had made a particularly good cast. "We catch permit this week, mon. I theenk so. Put me ahead of Pops. Yah." The guides took their competition very seriously.

In the afternoons we waded the flats and hunted schools of bonefish working up the tide. We caught a few of them—marvelous swift fish.

But they weren't permit.

On the third morning while I was balanced up on the casting platform staring blindly at the gray choppy water, Taku whispered, "There's a tail, mon. Look."

I looked. "Where?" I said. "Dammit, I can't see anything."

"There," said Andy. "I see it. Ten o'clock."

I looked hard and saw nothing. I cast in the ten o'clock direction anyway, and Taku yelled, "No, mon. To the left."

So I picked up and cast more to the left. "Right, mon!" said Taku.

I obediently picked up again and cast to the right.

"No, mon!" said Taku, exasperation dripping from his voice. "Oh, mon, you gotta—yes! Hit heem!"

A Slam for Taku

I felt the pull, hauled back, and a few seconds later a hundred yards of backing had zinged off my reel. The permit did not swim with quite the blazing speed of a bonefish, nor did it jump like a tarpon. It simply took line, and I could not slow it down. So I hung on, applying as much pressure as I dared, and after a while it turned and made a wide arc around the boat, and a little while later I was able to retrieve some backing before the fish took it away again.

Taku and Andy discussed it while I strained against the fish of my life. "How big?" said Andy.

"Big one," said Taku.

"This one'll put you up on Pops, eh?"

"Yeah, mon." He chuckled. "Poor ol' Pops."

I was remembering the first tarpon I ever hooked. I had bowed to all of his jumps, and I'd taken turns with him, losing and then regaining backing. I had him on for forty minutes before the hook pulled loose. Five more years passed before I finally actually boated my first tarpon.

That memory kept playing in my head while Andy and Taku chalked up this permit, the first one I'd ever hooked. I'd been tied to the fish for thirty minutes before I got all the backing onto my reel. Then we saw him silver and flash beside the boat. "We got heem, mon," said Taku. "He's beat."

Then my rod straightened and my line went limp.

"He's gone," I said.

I stripped in and found a pigtail where my crab fly used to be. A bad knot.

"Oh, jeez," said Andy.

Taku said nothing.

Later Andy explained that when Taku had yelled "left" my cast had been perfect. The tailing permit had turned toward my fly. When Taku then said "right" he'd meant, "Yes. Good cast." But I'd cast to the right, and the permit, now irritated by this strange crab that had appeared and then suddenly disappeared, had raced to where my new cast landed and gobbled my fly quickly before it could get away again.

I'd done just about everything wrong, beginning at the time I'd tied on my fly. I didn't deserve to catch that permit.

This did not console me, and it certainly didn't console Taku, who grumbled about it for the rest of the day.

On the fifth morning Taku yelled, "Feesh!" and Andy, up on the deck, said, "Okay! I see him." He cast, the underwater shadow turned, Andy set the hook, and they were connected. He boated the silvery flat-sided permit twenty minutes later, a little after ten A.M. "Twelve, thirteen pound," guessed Taku. "Nice one, mon." He and Andy shook hands. It was impossible to judge whose smile was broader. I took pictures and they released the permit.

"Now," I told Taku, "you're one up on Pops."

He grinned. "Ol' Pops, he be some pissed, mon."

Taku was relaxed now—no longer upset with me—and so were Andy and I. We poled the flats for the rest of the morning and spotted a few more fish, and neither Andy nor I did anything wrong, but we had no takes, and it hardly seemed to matter. We did more talking than fishing.

"What's your real name?" I asked Taku.

"William Johnson."

"What's 'Taku' mean?"

"North wind. In Creole."

"Why do they call you that?"

He shrugged. "I do not know, mon."

He showed me his hand, which was cramped into a permanent half-closed fist as if it had been shaped to fit around a pole. Years earlier, he told us matter-of-factly, someone had shoved a knife into his back in a Belize City bar. When he reached around to pull it out, he severed the tendons of his fingers on the blade. It used to be much worse, he said, before a wealthy American client arranged for an operation with a Houston hand surgeon. Now he could use it to pole a skiff and tie flies and make love and hold a can of Belikan beer.

"Do you have family?" I asked him.

"Yah, mon," he smiled. "Three little keeds and a wife and a girlfriend. They live in Belize City."

It didn't take much imagination to figure out that the native guides at places like Turneffe Flats were their society's elite. They had regular, well-paying jobs, they guided rich American fly fishermen, they traveled to Houston for hand surgery. They took their skills seriously. Competition for their jobs was fierce. They had to be the best.

Now Taku was the best of all. He had boated his fourth permit of the season.

But when we returned to the lodge for the noon meal, we learned that one of Pops's clients had landed a permit that morning, too. Pops and Taku were tied again.

After lunch, Taku was not smiling. He said to Andy, "You want to go for a slam?"

A Slam for Taku

The fly-fishing "grand slam" is catching a permit, a bonefish, and a tarpon in the same day. Achieving a slam is roughly equivalent to shooting two holes-in-one on the same round, or hitting four homers in a single game. It's been done. But it's always noteworthy. Lani Waller was the only angler ever to complete a slam at Turneffe Flats. His name had been engraved on a plaque that hung in the dining room of the lodge.

A good fly fisherman in the right place should be able to catch a bonefish. At the right time of year, and with some luck, he has a fair chance of also landing a tarpon that day. Most anglers who set out for a slam fail at the permit.

Andy is a skilled and experienced fisherman, and he had already done the hard part.

He arched his eyebrows at me. It would mean he'd be doing all the fishing, and we usually took equal turns. He worried about things like that.

"We've got to go for it," I said. "It's a chance to make history."

"Well, hell," he said to Taku, "I'd love to try for a slam. But what about tarpon?" April, we knew, was a month too early for tarpon in those waters. We hadn't even bothered looking.

Taku nodded. "I find tarpon, mon," he said. "We get Meester Bone first."

Easier said than done. The bonefish schools had been hard-fished for several months, and today they were especially skittish. Andy hooked one which promptly cut him off on coral. He found another school, cast to it, and a small barracuda out-muscled a bonefish for his fly, sending the bones into panicky flight. We walked a mile of bonefish flats, me with my camera and Andy and Taku squinting into the water. Then Taku stopped and pointed. "There," he said.

Andy began to strip line from his reel, and Taku said, "Hurry, mon. Big ray comin'. He'll spook the bones."

Andy cast, a bonefish took, and Andy held his rod high and sprinted across the knee-deep flat after the running fish. Taku and I ran behind him. Andy landed the fish, Taku estimated its weight at four pounds, I took pictures, and Andy released it. We jogged back to the skiff, anchored a mile behind us. It was nearly four in the afternoon. We had barely two hours to catch a tarpon.

"Well, now what?" said Andy as Taku cranked up the outboard.

"We go see Mr. Miller."

We weaved among the mangrove cays and skimmed across the big central lagoon. Then Taku cut the motor and we coasted up to a crude dock perched on the edge of a tiny island. A rickety hand-built windmill dominated this little patch of land. A couple of swamped dugout canoes were tied to the dock, and three mangy dogs crouched on the end barking at us. Coconut husks and sun-bleached conch shells littered the ground.

A young man about Taku's age emerged from the ramshackle hut beside the windmill and sauntered out onto the dock. He and Taku exchanged greetings in Creole. They talked briefly, then an older man came out of the hut. He was toothless and hairless and dark-skinned. He held a paperback novel closed on his forefinger.

Taku and he talked animatedly for several minutes. Then Taku bailed out one of the dugouts and tied it to the stern of our skiff. He climbed in and started up the motor. We towed the dugout across the lagoon.

"Mr. Miller and his boy, Carlos," said Taku. "They make coconut oil in their mill. I sometimes give them feeshhooks. They owe me."

He knew a little landlocked lagoon on one of the cays, he said. It held schools of snook and small tarpon. It could be fished only from the dugout. "You watch from the bank, mon," he said to me. "Only two men in canoe."

Taku beached the skiff. Then he and Andy dragged the heavy dugout though a hundred feet of jungle to the lagoon. As they shoved the canoe into the water, a crocodile slid lazily away from the shore.

I cleared my throat. "Um, are there many crocodiles?"

Taku shrugged. "Oh, yeah, mon. Plenty of crocs."

I thought about crocodiles—and spiders and lizards and tropical snakes. I thought about following along on the bank with my camera. "Maybe I'll just wait for you," I said.

Andy grinned at me.

I watched them push off. Taku paddled from the stern. Andy knelt up front. They had barely four inches of freeboard.

I returned to the skiff and waited. The sun was settling toward the horizon. They didn't have much time.

A half hour later I heard a whistle. I picked up my camera and jogged to the pond. They were just beaching the dugout.

"Well?" I said.

Andy grinned sheepishly. He reached into the bottom and held up a squirming little silvery fish. It was barely twelve inches long.

"Is that a . . . ?"

He shrugged. "A tarpon. Sort of."

"Eet's a tarpon, mon," said Taku.

"Then you got a slam," I said.

"Well, I don't know . . ."

"Congratulations!"

"Yeah, I guess."

I photographed the little fish in the fading light, and through the magnification of the lens it looked like a tarpon. Andy revived it gently and returned it to the lagoon. By the time we got back to the lodge, the sun had set.

At the bar, I held up my bottle of Belikan. "I've got an annoucement," I said.

The others turned to me.

"Andy got a slam today."

"Wait," said Andy quickly, before anyone could congratulate him. "It doesn't qualify. The tarpon was barely a foot long."

Doug, the manager of the lodge, decreed that the validity of Andy's slam should be decided democratically, by the group.

This called for a switch to rum-and-Cokes all around. Debate ensued. Andy argued that, while a twelve-incher might technically be considered a tarpon, such a puny specimen violated the spirit of the slam. Fish called "baby tarpon" go eight to ten pounds, and even fifty-pounders are considered small. A twelve-incher was simply not a legitimate tarpon.

The rest of us maintained that a fish is a damn fish, and there was nothing in the letter or the spirit of the slam that said anything about size. One bone, one permit, one tarpon, all caught on a fly in the same day. That's a grand slam.

Besides, the trek into the croc-infested lagoon in the dugout canoe made this little tarpon a worthy prize and more than offset its lack of heft.

Andy stubbornly insisted that his tiny tarpon was unworthy. All the others seemed willing to give it to him if he wanted it, but nobody wanted to force it on him.

He didn't want it, he said.

"Time out," I said. I grabbed Andy's arm and dragged him into a corner. "Listen," I said. "Just think about it for a minute."

"What's to think?"

"Whose slam is it, anyway?"

He frowned at me for a moment, then nodded. "It's Taku's, really, huh?"

"Right. You'll go home and practice medicine and nobody will know or care where you've been or whether you caught any fish. But guiding a client to a slam makes Taku a hero. It puts him on top of his heap down here. You want to deprive him of that?"

"No, I guess not. He did all the work, really. He found the permit. He knew where that . . . that tarpon lived."

"Then get over there and tell them you'll take it."

Which he did.

Andy's name was duly engraved under Lani Waller's on the Turneffe Flats grand-slam plaque. Andy insisted that William "Taku" Johnson's name be inscribed beside his.

24

Sam's Ear

"It sure don't feel like fall's ever going to to get here," Keith said, waving his hand at the roadside foliage, still lush and green, as we towed his boat up Maine's winding Route 1 to the Kennebec River. "No frost on the goldenrod, no crimson maples in the swamps. It don't even smell right."

"And bird season's only three weeks off," I said.

"Provided they don't close the woods," said Sam from the back seat. "Rumor has it they might. Forest fire danger and all."

"Yeah, we could sure use some rain," said Keith, "Anyway, they're saying the river's full of migrating stripers, so maybe the seasons are changing. Be nice to intercept a few big cows on their way south, put an exclamation point on this fishing season and get on to shooting some woodcock."

The summer-long drought had continued into September. We'd had no significant rainfall since Memorial Day, and this was another in an endess series of cloudless days.

We launched the boat and headed toward the mouth of the Kennebec. Sam and I started to rig up our fly rods while Keith steered. A hot dry wind was blowing directly upriver.

"Sink tips," said Sam, who sometimes guided on the Kennebec. "The big cows are down deep. Tie on something big and white with lead eyes."

Keith turned into a sheltered cove. Sam pointed. Breaking fish. We coasted up to them, and Sam and I both had our lines in the air. My first cast had barely hit the water when my fly stopped. "Got one," I mumbled.

"Schoolie," said Sam instantly.

He was right. Small stripers pull hard. We never sneer at them. But we weren't after eighteen-inchers.

If that fish belonged to a school, his classmates were playing hookey, because we got no more strikes in that cove. We headed back to the main channel. Keith ran the motor and trolled something big and ugly on his spinning rod while Sam and I double-hauled our heavy sink-tips toward the rocks and into the rips. Down toward the estuary the hot dry wind blew harder. We saw no breaking fish. We tried to fish the water, hot spots that Sam knew, the holes and eddies and current convergences where baitfish stacked up and where he'd had luck before. We had no hits.

Two men casting sink-tip lines from a small boat into a hard quartering wind invites trouble. It was inevitable that one of us would find flesh with a weighted 2/O saltwater streamer. It happened to be my streamer and Sam's ear.

"Ow," he observed quietly. "You got me."

I put down my rod and looked. "No blood," I said.

"Did you debarb it?"

"I always debarb my flies," I said. I cautiously wiggled the big streamer that hung from the top flap of his ear. "That hurt?"

"Nah," he grunted.

"Well," I said, "I don't think I debarbed this one. It's in over the barb and it's not moving."

"Gotta push it all the way through, then," said Sam, who proceeded—very gingerly—to do just that.

It was hard to watch. "Hurt?" I asked stupidly.

"Nope," he muttered through clenched teeth. "It's numb."

I noticed a tear squeeze out of his left eye.

He suddenly grunted, and the barb broke through. I cut it off above the barb, pushed the fly back through the way it had gone in, swabbed Sam's pierced ear with iodine from our first-aid kit, and sat down. "I'm sorry, man," I said.

"Hey, it could've just as well been me nailing you."

"No. It was stupid, both of us trying to cast at the same time. I wasn't paying attention. Sink-tips in the wind? Stupid."

"Nobody's fault," said Sam. "Forget it."

"I could've got you in the eye or something."

"Well, you didn't. So we're lucky. Anyway, I should've been wearing my hard-brimmed hat. I always wear that hat."

"Yeah, okay," I mumbled. "It's your fault, then."

"You take the bow for a while," said Sam.

"No," I said. "You go ahead."

Sam shrugged and began to cast. I sat on the middle seat, reeled up, and took down my rod.

"What're you doing?" said Keith.

I shrugged. "I've had enough, that's all."

Sam turned to me. "Just because we had an accident—"

"That's not really it. I'm just ready for fall to get here. I want to go bird hunting."

Sam's Ear

"If we don't get some rain," said Sam, "there won't be any hunting season this year."

The next night I cleaned and sorted a year's tangle of fishing gear and stowed it away. Then I took my shotguns from their cases, wiped them off, peered through their barrels, mounted them to my shoulder, and swung on imaginary woodcock corkscrewing through my den. Then I wiped them again and put them back.

I sat in my big chair. I patted my lap and Burt, my Brittany, hopped up. I scratched his muzzle and told him to start giving serious thought to bird smells. I told him how the stripers had apparently gone south, and how the woodcock should soon start following them down from Nova Scotia, and how I'd impaled Sam's ear with a 2/O Deceiver, and how I took that as a sure sign that it was time to move on to the next season.

That's when the phone rang. It was Art. "The Merrimack's full of stripers," he said. "I was out a couple days ago and—"

"No," I said.

"Huh?"

"No, I don't want to go fishing. Far as I'm concerned, fishing season's over. I nailed Sam in the ear yesterday. I just finished

putting my fishing stuff away for the winter. Now I'm just waiting to go hunting."

"Too bad," said Art. "They were breaking all over the river.
We caught 'em on poppers. Some pretty big ones, too. It was
better than that time we had back in June."

"Better than June?" I said. "That was a helluva good day."

"This was better."

"The fish were pretty much gone from the Kennebec."

"Sure," said Art. "They're moving south. They're here."

"They were really breaking all over the river?"

"Everywhere."

I said nothing.

"How's six-thirty tomorrow morning?" said Art.

"Sam didn't utter a peep," I said. "It must've hurt like hell. I
could've put out his eye."

"Wanna meet me at the ramp?"

"Okay," I said. "I guess so."

Black clouds hung low and dark and heavy over the
Merrimack. The air was still and moist and salty and the water
was flat and black and the muffled clang of a distant bell buoy
echoed through the mist. I rigged up my seven-weight with a
floating line and a debarbed popper.

"Watch out for me," I told Art as we pulled away from the ramp. "I stick hooks into people."

"We've fished together for close to forty years," he said. "You haven't stuck me yet. Anyway, I—look!"

He pointed to a swarm of gulls that were circling and diving a hundred yards ahead of us. Under them the water was spurting into the air.

"Hit it," I said.

He gunned the motor, then cut it, and as we drifted up to the school I had my line in the air, casting over the bow, very aware of Art in the stern.

My popper hit the water. I made it gurgle and it disappeared in a swirl. From behind me I heard Art grunt. I turned. His rod was bowed. Doubles on our first casts.

They were twin schoolies, small ones, sixteen-inchers, but they pulled harder than any sixteen-inch trout or bass, and when I released my fish and looked up, the air was full of birds and the water was churning with swirls and splashes as far as I could see. Every cast brought a slash and a strike, and we drifted with the tide and caught stripers steadily for two hours. Neither of us rammed a hook into the other's ear, and we didn't even notice when it started raining.

The fish disappeared abruptly and without warning. We cast for ten minutes without seeing a swirl or getting a strike. It was raining hard.

"It's over," said Art. "The tide turned, and that's that."

"Good," I said. I sat down, reeled up, and took down my rod.

Art peered up at the sky. "Lots of rain coming," he said. "This is our line storm. Cold front behind it. Yesterday it was summer. Tomorrow it'll be fall, and the stripers'll be gone."

"Hunting season," I said. "The woods will be wet. There'll be water in the brooks. The leaves will turn and there'll be frost on the goldenrod. The woodcock will come down."

"Now you can stow away your fishing gear."

"I did that once," I said. "Thanks for making me do it again. Now I don't have to think about Sam's ear all winter."

25

Making Peace with the Battenkill

I had fished the Battenkill just once before. Like Thoreau's fishermen, I'd caught nothing and had felt unlucky and poorly paid for my time.

I returned twenty years later determined, this time, to catch a worthy trout on a dry fly and thus make my peace with this fabled Vermont river—an undertaking, I realized, that others considered the work of a lifetime. I had no illusions. Everyone knows the Battenkill is one of the world's most challenging trout streams.

I talked to the clerks at Orvis in Manchester, and the proprietor of the little fly shop over the New York border, and the other anglers I enountered along the river, and even the groundskeeper at the inn in Arlington where I stayed. They talked mostly about insects. The Hendricksons had come and gone. A few blue-winged olives were hatching—not enough to interest the trout. Whatever significant mayfly would come next in the annual sequence had not yet appeared. Small tan-colored caddis flies were emerging toward dark and small trout were chasing them. There were midges. Small fish might eat them, but worthy Battenkill trout ignore midges.

One hesitates to ask another fisherman to divulge the location of a hot spot. Such knowledge is, and should be, earned. Along the Battenkill, I learned, a hot spot is defined as a place where a single large trout was once seen. If he was caught, it was most likely on a nightcrawler, and he would be killed and taken home by the person who had caught him—and that trout no longer lived in the river.

So I scouted for places where I, if I were a worthy trout, might choose to live, pieces of river that offered sanctuary from predators, protection from heavy currents, and a ready food source. I found dark runs against undercut banks. I found pools where the river widened below a chute of quickwater. I found long flats separated by riffly runs.

I discovered that the Battenkill has very little water that *doesn't* look as if it would harbor worthy trout.

I also discovered that very few worthy trout live there.

On the first day I explored a section of the river that a young clerk at Orvis called "the Jungle." I quickly saw why. The river's banks grow thick and tangly and impenetrable to a man wearing a vest festooned with dangling gadgets and carrying a nine-foot fly rod. Trees arch over the water, leaving it in permanent shadow. The only way to navigate is to wade the riverbed itself, where the Battenkill tumbles over slick softball-sized rocks that look bronze through the faintly tea-stained water. The river runs north to south over a sequence of long shallow stairs—riffle, run, pool, flat, riffle.

The sun dappled it here and there as I edged upstream. Warblers flittered in the May foliage, which glowed in vibrant young shades of pale green and yellow. Pink and crimson and white wildflowers sprouted along the riverbank.

I've fished many of America's most beautiful trout rivers: Nelson's and Armstrong's spring creeks in Montana's Paradise Valley, the South Fork of the Snake and the Middle Fork of the Salmon in Idaho, the limestone creeks of Pennsylvania, the Green River's Flaming Gorge in Utah, the South Platte's Cheesman Canyon in Colorado, not to mention the dozens of little streams that flow through the creases of Vermont's Green Mountains. None is more beautiful than the Battenkill.

I'm certain that you don't need to be a fisherman to recognize this beauty. But an angler searching for trout sees and appreciates it differently. We engage rivers more intensely and study them more critically. Many of them hold spooky, selective trout. Catching these fish demands knowledge and finesse, patience and luck. I have caught worthy trout from beautiful rivers, and it seems to make the rivers even more beautiful.

I worked my slow way upstream without even stringing up my rod. I could have fished the water blindly—there were plenty of likely looking places. I could have dredged the bottom of some of those holes and runs with weighted nymphs or caddis pupa imitations. That was the Orvis clerk's recommendation.

But I had come to the Battenkill to cast dry flies to rising trout. So I paused at the bottom of each long flat and squinted at the water's surface, searching for the dimple of a feeding trout. Then I edged along the bank, careful—though not always careful enough—to avoid sending ripples across the water. And I paused again at the head of each pool to stare at the choppy run that fed it.

A mile and a few hours after I had entered the river I rounded a bend. A long stretch of flat water curved upstream into the Jungle. And there against the left bank I saw the widening rings that I had been looking for. I stood motionless, and a minute or two later the rings appeared again. From where I stood I couldn't estimate the size of the fish that made those rings. Large trout tend to feed delicately, barely pricking the river's surface with their nose to sip insects. Small trout sometimes don't look much different.

I noticed a few caddis flies fluttering above the river. I snatched one and held it in my hand. Tan wings and olive body, about size sixteen. I found a match for it in my fly box and knotted it to my 6X tippet. Then I moved into position, a cautious stalk that ended with me kneeling painfully on the cobbled riverbottom in calf-deep water thirty feet downstream and to the side of my target trout. I waited that way until he rose again, and when he did I waited some more, merging my rhythm with his, until I felt he was prepared to rise again.

My cast was true. My fly settled softly on the water four feet upstream of him and drifted down, and then it disappeared into the dimple of his rise.

I tightened on him to set the hook. And then I laughed aloud. With the lift of my nine-foot rod, the fish came skittering across the surface of the water toward me. I stripped him in and held him in my hand. With his tail against the base of my thumb, his nose barely extended beyond my fingertips. A six-incher, by the fisherman's generous estimate. An altogether tiny trout.

But I had the good sense to admire him. He glittered in my hand like a gold nugget, perfectly camouflaged for the riverbottom where he lived. His red spots glowed like droplets of fresh blood. He was a perfect miniature of the worthy brown trout I sought. He had been born in this river, the descendent of the European browns that were brought to America in the nineteenth century and first introduced into the Battenkill in the 1930s.

This little trout had started as one of a million fertilized eggs on the gravelly streambottom. He had hatched. His parents did not eat him, nor did other cannibalistic trout, nor did herons, kingfishers, or ospreys. He had escaped disease and winterkill. For two years he had managed to swallow insects and avoid swallowing a worm with a hook in it, and against all the odds he had survived.

Nowadays a wild New England trout, however tiny, is always a miracle. Only a lout would fail to pause to admire one of them before slipping him gently back into the river.

I explored the loop of river between the first two bridges on Route 313 in Arlington on the second day. The sun glittered in a high sky and a sharp breeze blew the bugs off the water. I saw no rising trout. I spent most of the day sitting on streamside boulders watching sunlight ricochet off the riffles. After a few pleasant hours of idle watching and daydreaming, I succumbed to a pragmatic impulse and tied on a pair of weighted nymphs— a pheasant tail, which imitates many immature mayfly species, and a tan caddis pupa. I drifted them along a current seam that reminded me of places where I had caught worthy trout from Montana's Bighorn and Alberta's Bow rivers.

For all I could tell, not a trout lived in this Battenkill pool.

Toward dusk I made my way back to the bridge where I'd left my car. An elderly man was parked beside me. He was shucking off his waders. I asked after his luck first, so he was forced to admit he'd been skunked before I had to. He seemed cheerful about it. No bugs, no trout, he shrugged. A simple equation. He lived nearby, fished for a few hours just about every day, got skunked regularly.

It happens less regularly to me because I generally don't fish in rivers as idiosyncratic as the Battenkill. I don't like to spend ten hours on a stream without so much as a single strike. It makes me believe that there's something wrong—either with the river, or with me. I prefer to blame myself. I don't want things to be wrong with rivers.

I was reluctant to leave. My friend told me that he'd once taken a sixteen-inch brown trout from the Battenkill. That was his biggest. It had happened four years earlier. I confessed that I'd caught a six-incher the previous day. He smiled. He said he'd had plenty of days when he hadn't done that well.

I removed my waders, took down my rod, and went up to the bridge for a final look at the river. Swallows had begun to swoop close to the water, and a few caddisflies swarmed in the air. Then I saw the rise of a trout, and as I watched I saw two more. One of them appeared to be heftier than my six-incher.

I returned to the car. "There's a few rising below the bridge," I told my new friend.

He smiled. "Why don't you go catch one?"

"I guess I will." I restrung my rod and stuck a box of caddis imitations into my shirt pocket. I didn't bother climbing back into my waders.

I stood on the river's edge below the bridge, and now there were half a dozen fish feeding steadily, splashing at the insects that fluttered over the water. My fly was invisible on the dark water. I cast upstream of a feeding trout, and if he rose when my fly was on the water, I lifted my rod. A couple of times I guessed fish had splashed at my fly, but I didn't hook them.

As the dusk gathered, they began to feed more hungrily. Now I had at least a dozen actively rising fish in front of me. I cast frantically, amateurishly, first to this one, and then, when another rose nearby, I'd interrupt the drift of my fly, lift my line, and cast to him. Perhaps some of these were worthy trout, although I couldn't judge.

Then I caught one. He did not come skittering in over the surface, but neither did he slog heavily at the end of my line. I landed him easily and measured him against the markings on my rod. His nose failed by an inch to reach the one-foot mark. He was a brook trout, a species native to the Battenkill. Perhaps this one was a descendant of those that settled here after the glaciers retreated. More likely his ancestors were hatchery trout that were heavily stocked a century ago.

Either way, I knew he was another wild trout, a survivor born in the river. It's been many years since hatchery trout have been dumped into the Battenkill. I revived him carefully and slipped him back into the river.

"How big?"

I turned. My friend had been watching from the bridge.

"About eleven inches," I said.

"Brown?"

"Brookie."

"Three-year old fish," he said. "Brook trout don't live much longer here. That's a really nice brookie for the Battenkill. About as big as they get."

On most of the Western rivers I fish, an eleven-inch trout would be an embarrassment. I realized I was still taking the measure of the Battenkill.

In Arlington, the river takes a right turn and flows east to west into New York, where, for some reason, they call it the Batten Kill. On the third day, I prowled this stretch, which for several miles meanders between Route 313 and a dirt road. I drove the dirt road and stopped wherever I found a pulloff. More beautiful trout water and another sparkling May day— high blue sky, pillowy white clouds, that same persistent breeze. Perfect for photography, but not the sort of day that encouraged mayflies to hatch or trout to rise.

I saw more fishermen than I had the previous two days. Most of them were using spinning rods, and I did not try to engage them in conversation. They were probably pleasant people. But spin fishermen do not study insects, and they ignore rising fish. They toss their lures into likely-looking currents. When trout are not feeding on insects, a man with a spinning rod will out-fish a fly caster. But during an insect hatch, the fly fisherman has the advantage.

I could not learn anything from these fishermen.

In the morning, as I sat beside the river watching the water, a hen turkey ambled down to the bank across from me. I didn't move, but she saw me anyway and ran awkwardly into the bushes. Toward dusk a whitetail doe waded into the head of the pool I was fishing.

In between, I caught two miniature brown trout and one finger-sized brookie. I guessed that all three, laid head to tail, would barely stretch beyond the length of my eleven-inch brookie. I had again avoided being skunked.

But I had not encountered the worthy trout I sought. I knew they lived here. Most Battenkill stories—both those in literature and those exchanged among fishermen—invariably mention the river's "lunker browns." These wily old trout show themselves rarely. Most of them are caught in the early spring by bait fish-ermen. But now and then a persistent fly fisherman finds one that has slipped from its sanctuary among submerged roots to sip insects. Occasionally one of these big browns will eat the angler's fly. Usually it breaks the slender tippet. But some are landed. They might weigh five pounds or more. The largest brown trout ever taken from the Battenkill weighed over twelve pounds. But that happened fifty years ago.

Fishing in the first four miles of the river after it enters New York is restricted to flies and artificial lures. Only three trout of ten inches or longer may be killed per angler per day. Compared with the regulations on many of Montana's blue-ribbon trout streams (flies with barbless hooks only, strictly catch-and-release), New York's rules are primitive. But compared with Vermont, where all methods are legal and anglers may kill twelve trout per day, New York's management of this section of the Battenkill is perfectly enlightened.

After three days on the river, I had seen enough to understand that the Battenkill has the potential to match some of the most productive trout rivers I have fished. Its pure water—a mix from the springs that rise in the Taconics to the west and warmer surface runoff from the Green Mountains to the east—rarely exceeds seventy degrees, which is ideal for brown trout and tolerable for brookies. The alkaline riverbed encourages weed and insect growth. Trout reproduce abundantly here. But they are overfished, overharvested, and undermanaged.

Words such as "technical" and "challenging" are often applied to the Battenkill. Such descriptions are misleading. They imply that a sufficiently skilled angler can succeed here. I have talked with enough excellent fly fishermen who know the Battenkill to understand that this gorgeous, trouty river simply does not offer even the superior angler a fair challenge. Its fish are scarcer and smaller and more skittish than the quality of this river promises.

For a trout fisherman, at least, it's a tragic waste. Lee Wulff, perhaps history's most famous fly fisherman, lived in Shushan, New York, on the banks of the Battenkill for twenty years. When he moved, he blamed the deterioration of the fishing.

My best chance to encounter my worthy brown trout, I decided, lay in that four-mile stretch over the New York border. A waitress told me that "lots of big trout" were taken there, although on the Battenkill's scale, I had no idea what a "big trout" might be, or how many constituted "lots."

I parked by the covered bridge at the very end of the restricted four miles. There were no other cars there, which promised the solitude I sought, but which I nevertheless interpreted as an ominous sign. How good could the fishing be if none of the wise locals came here?

Rain clouds obscured the mountains and mist hung over the river. The air was still and heavy and damp. A good day for insects. A good day for a worthy brown trout to come out to eat them.

A good day for a fly fisherman.

I waded across the river above the covered bridge and picked my way upstream, moving slowly, watching the water. It was, I quickly learned, an excellent day for insects. Mosquitoes clouded around my head. But there were caddisflies, too, and a few assorted mayflies—large dun-colored ones with smoky wings that might have been leftover Hendricksons, smaller brownish ones with mottled wings that I guessed were March Browns, and tiny blue-winged olives. Drifting on the water, too, were some mayfly spinners, spent and dying after their reproductive exertions.

There were enough insects, I guessed, to interest a worthy trout. But I crept upstream a mile or more without seeing a single ring on the water. The mist became a steady, soft rain.

I rounded a bend and paused at the tail of a flat that extended so far upstream that the mist blurred its head. The left bank, I saw, was the deep one. Some dead timber had collected there and a big oak grew at an angle over the water. Its branches swooped so low that they nearly ticked its surface.

I sat on a rock. Here, I decided, I would take my stand. In four days I had not seen a more likely lair for a worthy trout. I would sit here all day if necessary to wait for him to show himself.

A ring appeared near the tailout, not thirty feet from me. I could cast to him without moving. I waited, and when the trout rose again I knew he was a small one, another six-incher. I ignored him.

Gradually more rings began to show on the glass-smooth surface of the long pool. I sat quietly in the misty rain and watched them. Small trout, all of them, but even so, they fed cautiously. A minute or more separated each quick foray to the surface. On this absolutely flat water, fooling even one of these six-inchers would take precision and luck. It was tempting.

But going after one of those little trout would have been a concession to the river, and I wasn't ready to admit that the Battenkill had beaten me. I would hold out for a worthy trout.

An hour passed before I saw the unmistakable black nose. On the Henrys Fork and the Bighorn I had learned to measure a surface-feeding trout by the size of his nose.

Here on the Battenkill I'd found a "toad." I didn't move for ten minutes, the interval it took him to come to the surface three times. He rose in precisely the same place each time, about two feet directly upstream from the uppermost sweeping branch of the arching oak tree. The only way I could float a fly over him was from the side and upstream.

His delicate riseform suggested he had selected spinners to eat. They drifted inert on the water's surface membrane, easy pickins for an energy-conscious trout. I saw two kinds of spinners on the water: large rust-colored ones and smaller olives. Knowing the perversity of large trout, I guessed this one had selected the olives.

I found a good match in my fly box and tied it to my long wispy tippet. My hands, I noticed, trembled just a little. After three days, the Battenkill had showed me a worthy trout. Now it was up to me. The odds, I knew, were slim. Getting a drag-free drift would require a tricky reach cast and a big upstream mend, and I figured I'd have only one chance to get it right. And even if I hooked this fish, he would bolt to what I assumed was his lair under the tangled timber against the bank. My tippet was too slender. It would snap if I tried to hold him back. Otherwise he would wrap me and surely break me off.

Perhaps not. When they're hooked, large trout sometimes shoot directly upstream, or try to slog it out in midriver, or exhaust themselves by jumping repeatedly. I might get lucky.

I focused on the first challenge, which was to wade into position to make my cast. A careless step would send warning waves across the quiet pool, and the trout would dart back to his hideout for the rest of the day. So I moved downstream and crossed in the quick water of the pool's tailout. Then I climbed the bank and pushed through the alder tangles to a spot directly across from the fish. I paused there until his nose showed again. Then I slipped down the bank and into the water.

The river spread one hundred feet wide here, and my trout lay about ten feet from the far bank. To drop an accurate cast over him, I'd need to wade to midstream. There was virtually no discernible current. I began to edge forward, shuffling my feet slowly, wary of making ripples. He rose again. I was closer, now, and I saw the size of his nose more clearly and mentally compared it with noses I had judged on other rivers. A sixteen-incher, at least. Maybe eighteen. Not a Battenkill five-pounder. But a most worthy trout.

I had to resist the impulse to cast. I was still too far from him. One careless presentation would spook him. So I waded cautiously forward. He showed his nose again. He had established a rhythm now, and I had learned it.

A hollow thunk echoed from somewhere upstream, but it barely registered. I was focused on my trout. I was almost there.

And then the man in the canoe materialized out of the mist. He paddled placidly down the middle of my pool, halfway between me and the place where my trout had been rising.

"Any luck?" he asked cheerfully.

I shook my head. "Nope."

"Say," he said. "You got the time?"

I glanced at my watch. "Three-fifteen."

"Thanks." He waved. "Well, good luck, then."

I watched the canoe's bow waves roll toward the banks. The canoe became a shadow before the mist enveloped it. I waded to shore.

Three-fifteen. I had parked at the covered bridge at nine. In effect, I had been stalking that trout for more than six hours.

I waded carelessly back to the car. There was no need to worry about my waves spooking fish. Every worthy trout in the river had already been sent scurrying by that one man in his canoe.

I stopped at the diner on the state line for coffee. The guy behind the counter squinted at my waders and said, "Been fishin', huh?"

I nodded.

"Do any good?"

I smiled and shook my head.

"Listen," he said. "Out behind the field here they were jumpin' all over the place last night. Nice ones, too. Eight, ten inches, some of 'em. You oughta try it there."

"Thanks," I said. "I appreciate it."

He gave me a free refill, and when I stood to go he said, "Just take that dirt road there and you can park beside the field."

I did. The river ran dark and deep along a granite ledge overhung by hemlocks. It was beautiful and peaceful in the mist, and I spotted the rings of a few rising trout and caught two of them. They weren't the "nice" ones the guy at the diner had seen, but they were five or six inches long, beautiful miniature Battenkill brown trout.

It was, as Thoreau said it was supposed to be, a "clarifying process." I fished until dark, casting rhythmically, no longer in search of a worthy trout, and finally the sediment of fishing sank all the way to the bottom and my purpose became pure.

And so I made my peace with the Battenkill.